D1569107

TRANSFORMING
San Antonio

TRANSFORMING
San Antonio

. . . .

AN INSIDER'S VIEW OF THE AT&T CENTER, TOYOTA, THE PGA VILLAGE, AND THE RIVER WALK EXTENSION

Nelson W. Wolff

FOREWORD BY
HENRY CISNEROS

Trinity University Press
SAN ANTONIO

Published by Trinity University Press
San Antonio, Texas 78212

Jacket design by Erin Kirk New
Book design by BookMatters, Berkeley

⊗ The paper used in this publication meets the minimum
requirements of the American National Standard for
Information Sciences—Permanence of Paper for Printed
Library Materials, ANSI Z39.48-1992.

Library of Congress Cataloging-in-Publication Data
Wolff, Nelson W., 1940–
    Transforming San Antonio / Nelson W. Wolff ;
foreword by Henry Cisneros.
        p.   cm.
    SUMMARY: "Bexar County judge and former mayor
    Nelson Wolff gives an insider's view of four major
    developments—the San Antonio Spurs' AT&T
    Center, Toyota, the PGA Village, and the River Walk
    extension—that are transforming the city" —*Provided
    by publisher.*
    Includes an index.
    ISBN 978-1-59534-046-7 (hardcover : alk. paper)
    1. Urban renewal—Texas—San Antonio.
    2. City planning—Texas—San Antonio.
    I. Title.
    HT177.S36W65   2008
    307.3′41609764351—dc22   2008000991

12   11   10   09   08   C   5   4   3   2   1

After the tumultuous events of the Mexican Revolution, which expelled Spain from North America, and the Texas War of Independence, which resulted in the Lone Star Republic and eventually the state of Texas, San Antonio entered a phase as the largest and most important city in Texas. It was a commercial center for ranching, for trade, and for military suppliers during the Civil War. By the end of the nineteenth century it was regarded as one of the fast-growing, fast-living cities of the new West, on par with New Orleans and San Francisco for modern conveniences and civic achievements. The city was noted nationally for its gas streetlights, trolley cars, quality hotels, and civic spirit.

In the 1920s and 1930s, with Houston's emergence as a national petroleum center and Dallas's evolution into a regional financial capital, both cities surpassed San Antonio in population. But San Antonio ushered in a new phase as host to important military facilities. Because of its many days of good flying weather annually and the imperatives of World War II, the city would eventually house seven military bases. Military and civil service wages and federal contracting expenditures rippled across every sector of the economy and for more than half a century provided a foundation as the city's largest economic sector. Because of the military leaders who were posted at the city's bases, San Antonio developed a national reputation. The careers and lifelong memories of such American notables as Theodore Roosevelt, Douglas MacArthur, Charles Lindbergh, and Dwight Eisenhower were shaped by their time in San Antonio.

In the postwar years it was clear that federal expenditures could not sustain the needs of the area's diverse and growing

Foreword

CITIES FUNCTION MUCH LIKE living organisms. They have life histories. They grow in specific locales for reasons of geography, economics, and culture. Over decades they are spurred by opportunities that propel them forward and are buffeted by forces that set them back. The ebb and flow of city growth can be described as phases of life.

San Antonio's history can be generally characterized by observable phases of surge and plateau. The area's first phase began with the birth of the pueblo as a military and religious outpost. The site was selected by a Spanish expedition inspired by what chroniclers called an oasis of clear flowing water and cottonwood shade amid the heat and parched earth of what is now South Texas. Those characteristics had made the San Antonio River basin a focal point for the nomadic indigenous people who camped along the riverbanks for hundreds of years. The Spanish located five missions along the river and organized the administrative center of a region that extended to what is today Wyoming. San Antonio served this role from 1691 to 1810, during which its character, physical patterns, architectural themes, and cultural spirit were formed.

population. City leaders defined a new phase by wisely investing public and private resources to build the city's tourist attractions—highlighted by a world's fair, HemisFair '68—and to attract the University of Texas Health Science Center to the fledgling South Texas Medical Center. The city's leaders launched a well-organized economic development effort through the San Antonio Economic Development Foundation, matched it with city governmental capacities, and opened the doors to a broader and more inclusive concept of economic opportunity. These leadership commitments effectively added two major components— tourism and the biosciences—to the region's economic engine and created a public consensus on progress that is still with us today. The city's amenities expanded to include the San Antonio Spurs, the Alamodome, River Walk extensions, new parks, university expansions, and downtown improvements.

Now, in the first decade of the twenty-first century, San Antonio is prepared to enter another phase. The new platform builds on the accomplishments of the last thirty years. And because those accomplishments add up to a critical mass, a measurably higher order of capabilities, they are pushing the city to a new level. Higher goals—possibilities once unthinkable—are now achievable. The city is home to the largest telecommunications company in the nation—AT&T; home to the nation's largest petroleum refinery—Valero; headquarters for the nation's largest radio broadcast company—Clear Channel Communications; site of the automotive manufacturing complex with the world's largest physical footprint—Toyota Manufacturing of Texas; home to USAA, one of the nation's largest mutual insurance companies, with a headquarters building that has the largest office square footage west of the Pentagon; and headquarters for H-E-B, one of the nation's largest grocery chains and largest privately owned companies. In addition, the health care and biosciences sector—comprised of biomedical education, research, clinical care, pharmaceuticals, and medical equipment companies—employs over 100,000 people.

These economic bulwarks—along with other major businesses headquartered here, such as KCI, Tesoro, Rackspace Managed Hosting, and Frost Bancshares—make possible cultural amenities, public improvements, entertainment offerings, educational facilities, and philanthropic gifts that together raise the city's overall quality of life. Because of the sheer magnitude of these cumulative investments, the city is poised for a new surge that will make it one of the nation's most consistently growing cities in the new century.

Nelson Wolff is precisely the right person to describe the public decisions and private investments that define this new potential. His natural skills as a historian and writer alone make his narrative insightful and valuable. But his extraordinary abilities as a leader and his temperament as a unifier have made him the only person who has in succession been the principal decision maker for the city and the county as economic advances like AT&T and Toyota and community amenities like the AT&T Center, the PGA Village, and the River Walk extension were formulated. He has been in the perfect position to help guide these decisions and now to share their inner workings with the rest of us.

Even more important, Nelson's insider view can help us understand how to leverage these successes into the work that still needs to be done. Daunting challenges remain—to assure the city's long-term water supply, to develop a twenty-first-century airport, to improve education at all levels, and to continue to enhance the quality of life and raise the standard of living for every citizen. If the decisions described in *Transforming San Antonio* prove to be the foundation for the continuing progress we need, they will be widely appreciated as far-reaching and wise in the years to come.

Henry Cisneros

County Government Comes into Its Own

DURING HIS TERM AS MAYOR of San Antonio, from 1981 to 1989, Henry Cisneros changed the ceremonial office of mayor into a powerhouse and used that power to make the city of San Antonio a driving force in economic development. His legacy allowed the community to continue building a strong economic foundation.

In the first seven years since the turn of the twenty-first century, four major economic development projects have further solidified that foundation. Never before has the city experienced so many diverse major initiatives in such a compressed time frame. The AT&T Center, the PGA Village, Toyota, and the thirteen-mile San Antonio River Walk extension have already dramatically influenced the area's environmental policy, geographical growth, governmental relations, tourism industry, and arts and culture. These initiatives are leading us into a new era of economic prosperity.

All four are public-private partnerships, and the public sector includes not one but two strong local partners. The last nine years have brought a major shift in the role of county government, leading it to play a critical part in these public-private partnerships.

Having the county as a strong and equal partner with the city is healthy for the community. Two strong local governments working together have had a profound effect on the community's development. One can pick up the other when it stumbles, as the county did when the city fumbled the ball for the San Antonio Spurs.

I write this story from my perspective as Bexar County judge, a post to which I was appointed by the Commissioners Court in May 2001 to succeed County Judge Cyndi Krier. She had resigned to become a member of the University of Texas Board of Regents. I was officially sworn in on May 8, three days after Ed Garza was elected mayor of San Antonio. Since my appointment I have been reelected county judge twice.

Going to the county after serving two terms as mayor of San Antonio in the early 1990s was a bit of a culture shock. I was accustomed to a hierarchical structure where power was concentrated with the city manager and the mayor. I soon found that in county government power was widely dispersed. After Krier handed me the gavel, she said: "You'll see that it's hard to find accountability. Everybody is responsible, and nobody is. To get anything meaningful done you'll have to get several independent powers in county government to agree with you."

Fragmented organization, as well as legislative and constitutional restrictions on its authority, left county government weak and extraneous. The 1877 Texas Constitution provided for a five-member Commissioners Court presided over by a county judge.

Commissioners Court has the authority to tax, set the county budget, and manage some aspects of county government. To counterbalance the court's authority, the constitution also established an array of elected officials, including county tax assessor-collector, sheriff, district clerk, county clerk, treasurer, district attorney, four constables, and numerous judges. Even though Commissioners Court funds each one of these offices, the elected officials hire and manage their own departments.

To further complicate matters, the district judges hire the auditor, adult probation director, and juvenile probation director. Three judges and two commissioners hire the purchasing agent.

These constitutional and legislative impediments traditionally relegated county government in urban areas to the backwaters of governance. With a home rule charter—which, as the name suggests, allows cities to create their own forms of government—cities in urban areas became the dominant local powers. In 1951 the City of San Antonio adopted its existing charter, which provided for a council-management form of government, centralizing all power with the city manager, mayor, and city council.

Krier was a ten-year veteran of the Texas Senate when she became county judge in January 1992. She stepped into this quagmire during my second year as mayor. While we worked well together, the city and county had little interaction. The city was the dominant local governmental entity, while county government appeared stuck in the nineteenth century. The county simply was not a player.

That began to change after I left office in 1995. Voters had amended the City Charter in 1991 to limit the mayor and council members to two 2-year terms, the severest term limits in the nation. I had a front-row seat to the change because I was elected mayor the same year. The initial effect was positive. That first city coun-cil included both seasoned veterans and new members with fresh ideas. But as the years passed, the term limits created a constant churn of mayors and council members. Many members resigned before their terms ended so they could run for a different office and, at the same time, help choose their replacements. Because of that, from 1991 to 2001 nine members were appointed, rather than elected, to council seats. The constant turnover resulted in inexperienced mayors and council members. It became clear that the voters had driven a stake into the heart of City Hall.

While City Hall politicians were going through a revolving door, the county commissioners, unhampered by term limits, were gaining years of experience. Krier joined the veteran court and set about strengthening county government. She enhanced Commissioners Court's role by bringing in more experienced pro-fessional staff who reported directly to the court. She hired Marcus Jahns, a former city assistant manager, to become the county's first budget officer. She hired four executive directors to report directly to the court. She increased salaries for top management positions and expanded the use of technology and e-government.

With these steps, she slowly took an outdated, fragmented government and molded it into an effective local entity. Then converging events left county government poised for a new expanded role. When the Texas legislature passed a bill in 1997 allowing major urban cities to build sports venues with a combi-nation of taxes, including the hotel-motel tax and sales tax, as well as fees on rental cars, tickets, and parking, it also provided that authority to the county. This allowed the county to step in with its plan for a new arena and the funding mechanism to support it.

A 1999 battle for a new arena for the Spurs was the county's shot over the mast of City Hall, signaling that it was about to emerge as a power player. The story of how wily veteran members of the Commissioners Court stiff-armed greenhorn council recruits while Krier stole the basketball from Mayor Howard Peak is fascinating. After that victory, county government emerged from the city's shadow and became a respected entity.

Even after Krier led the county's effort to win the right to build the new Spurs arena, most people were still confused about the county judge's role. On the way to the office the day after my appointment, I stopped at a restaurant for my usual sausage-biscuit sandwich. A lady who often waits on me said, "I'm so glad you were appointed judge. I've been wanting to divorce my husband for years." I had to explain that I was not that kind of judge.

Actually, I wasn't any kind of judge. Because of the increased complexity of running county government, county judges in urban areas have relinquished almost all their judicial duties. Instead they devote their time to running the county and presiding over Commissioners Court.

While the court shares power with other elected county officials in administering the judicial system, tax collection system, law enforcement, and jail, they retain some inherent powers. The court decides where and how to build roads, parks, drainage projects, and buildings. It determines all economic development projects and budget issues.

When I became county judge, I had the advantage of having served not only as a Texas representative and senator, but also as a city councilman and mayor. I became the first county judge who had also been mayor since Bryan Callaghan, who became mayor in 1885 and county judge in 1892.

I used the knowledge I had gained at City Hall to further strengthen Commissioners Court's role. I convinced the court to appoint my chief of staff, Seth Mitchell, to chair a county executive committee coordinating the work of all county departments. We created an economic development office headed by David Marquez. We strengthened our intergovernmental team by hiring Leilah Powell, Garza's top administrative assistant, to be our legislative liaison. We also hired Joe Aceves to head up our infrastructure services department. He had been director of the city's public works and the first San Antonio Water System president. We promoted David Smith to budget director and hired Aurora Sanchez to head up human services. We created the department of criminal jurisprudence, headed by Keith Carlton. I also brought in the well-connected community leader Julie Moke as my administrative assistant.

With our newly strengthened team, we joined as equal partners with the city to act in a number of important projects. Together we created the Metropolitan Partnership for Energy and the San Antonio Mobility Coalition. We contracted with the city to consolidate a number of governmental services. Garza and I worked together to submit to voters the first city-county joint bond program. All nine bond propositions, totaling $214 million, passed in November 2003 with strong percentages. They included parks, streets and roads, drainage, an emergency center, and an adult and juvenile probation facility.

But most important, over the last seven years I have had an extraordinary opportunity to participate in four major economic development projects that have become major building blocks—the AT&T Center, the PGA Village, Toyota, and the San Antonio River Walk extension.

One of the projects, the AT&T Center, which was financed by the hotel-motel tax and the car rental tax, will be paid off early, enabling the county to submit to voters the opportunity to invest in the San Antonio River Walk extension, a performing arts center, amateur sports facilities, and improvements to the AT&T Center, the Joe and Harry Freeman Coliseum, and the San Antonio Livestock Exposition facilities.

Krier was the dominant leader in securing the county's right to build the AT&T Center. I played a small part by overseeing the arena's construction after I was appointed county judge. For the first four years of my term, I worked with Garza on securing Toyota and the PGA Village. While he seemed a bit enigmatic to most people, I found him to be a solid partner with whom I really enjoyed working.

After Hardberger was elected mayor in 2005, I had the delightful privilege of working with him on numerous projects, including the River Walk extension. He came to the mayor's office with great experience, having served first as justice and then as chief justice of the Fourth Court of Appeals from 1994 to 2002. He has brought a renaissance to City Hall by hiring City Manager Sheryl Sculley from Phoenix. We are contemporaries as well as good friends.

With this understanding of county government's recent progress and its relationship to the city, let's turn to how San Antonio is entering a new era of economic prosperity.

ONE

·······················

The AT&T Center,
Home of the Spurs

THE AT&T CENTER, HOME of the Spurs, was a long time coming. The road that led to its construction began more than four decades ago. The story is worth telling because the events of those decades have profoundly impacted political careers, economic expansion, professional sports, and local government relations.

In 1962 a group of citizens founded San Antonio Fair, Inc., to originate an international fair. The following year I entered St. Mary's University School of Law, located downtown along the San Antonio River, fronting on College Street where the La Mansión del Rio hotel now stands. During my first year of law school, Lila Cockrell was elected to the San Antonio city council. Over the next five years, as chair of a council subcommittee that was the city's liaison to the fair's executive committee, she played an important role in the development of HemisFair '68.

As the fair was planned and constructed, I enjoyed studying on the banks of the river behind the school and frequenting two prominent businesses there. Some evenings we walked along the river to eat at Casa Rio, and on weekends we listened to Jim

Cullum's Happy Jazz Band at The Landing, a block downriver from the school.

By the time I completed law school in 1966, it was clear that the idyllic river bend would change forever. Plans were under way to relocate the school to the St. Mary's University campus on the west side of town. Around the river bend, a Hilton Hotel was under construction across the street from HemisFair Plaza. The river was being extended east to the new convention center on the HemisFair site.

On April 6, 1968, I attended the opening of the fair, which celebrated the confluence of civilizations in the Western Hemisphere. Cockrell was involved in numerous public events that day. She joined Gov. John Connally, Lady Bird Johnson, Mayor Walter W. McAllister, and other dignitaries as they toured the fair.

Exhibits from thirty-three nations were located in several pavilions. The 750-foot-high Tower of the Americas rose majestically above the fair, signifying a new San Antonio. Elevated walkways, a sky ride, a monorail, and boats on a lagoon made the fair an exciting place to visit. The grounds were also home to the new convention center and a theater later named in honor of Mayor Cockrell. A small arena attached to the convention center provided a place for larger conventions to assemble their delegates and a venue for concerts and other entertainment. At the time, no one understood the significance of the arena investment.

The six-month-long fair lost money, but it laid the groundwork for a thriving tourist industry. The convention center supported the development of numerous hotels, restaurants, and retail stores along the river.

While Cockrell and I attended the fair's opening, three others who would have political roles in the development of the AT&T Center—Henry Cisneros, Howard Peak, and Cyndi Krier—missed it. Cisneros was in his senior year at Texas A&M University, Krier was a senior at George West High School some 100 miles south of San Antonio, and Peak was attending the University of Texas. They each, however, attended the fair sometime that summer. Cisneros took a part-time job with the city, and Krier started her freshman year at Trinity University, which extended curfew hours so students could attend the fair. Peak, working that summer in Austin, came to the fair on weekends to drink a few beers at the House of Sir John Falstaff. Four of us eventually became mayors of San Antonio. Krier and I each served as county judge. Each of us would have an impact on the AT&T Center's evolution.

The small convention center arena saw little use until 1973, when businessman Red McCombs teamed up with stockbroker Angelo Drossos to lease the Dallas Chaparrals basketball team and move it to San Antonio. The Chaparrals, who were playing in the upstart American Basketball Association (ABA), had been struggling with poor attendance in Dallas. The investment was risky for McCombs, Drossos, and thirty-two other investors who put money in the team. It was questionable not only whether a professional basketball team would draw fans in San Antonio but also whether the league itself would survive. The twelve-team American Basketball Association had formed only six years earlier, in 1967, to compete against the well-established National Basketball Association.

McCombs and Drossos renamed the team the San Antonio Spurs and changed the team's colors from red, white, and blue to the now famous silver and black. The team played its first game in 1973 in the arena, which seated about 12,500 when configured for basketball.

A state senator at the time, I remember attending some of the first games with several other legislators. The fans exploded with shouts and applause for the Spurs. ABA games were more exciting than NBA games because the league utilized more wide-open offensive play and had invented the three-point field goal. During the first season, the Spurs began building a fan base with their winning record (45-39). When George Gervin, a future NBA Hall-of-Famer known as the Iceman, arrived in January 1974, the Spurs had their first superstar. They became one of the top teams in the ABA.

In 1976 the ABA failed. Cockrell, who had been elected mayor in 1975, worked with McCombs and Drossos to convince the NBA to incorporate the Spurs into their league. She sent attorney Pat Maloney to represent the city when NBA owners met in Florida to determine which ABA teams would be admitted. She played a key role when she told the NBA she would enlarge the arena to expand seating.

To the relief of the investors and the city, the NBA accepted the Spurs, along with the Denver Nuggets, Indiana Pacers, and New York Nets. These four ABA teams enlarged the NBA to twenty-two teams. Founded as the Basketball Association of America in 1946, the NBA grew in popularity during the 1960s when centers Bill Russell and Wilt Chamberlain created one of the greatest rivalries in team sports. By the time the Spurs joined, the NBA was becoming popular nationally, and the franchise became part of a storied league.

In 1977 Cockrell kept her promise to the NBA, raising the arena roof to accommodate 6,000 more seats. Fans filled the additional seats as the Spurs proved they could compete against the NBA's best players, capturing five division titles in their first seven years in the league.

In 1979 the NBA adopted the ABA's three-point field goal and opened up the game for more exciting play. That same year rookies Larry Bird and Magic Johnson entered the league. In 1984 Michael Jordan, the most exciting player in NBA history, joined the Chicago Bulls. Bird led the Boston Celtics to three titles, Johnson took the Los Angeles Lakers to five, and Jordan led the Bulls to six. With such stiff competition during the mid-1980s, the Spurs struggled, posting a four-year combined record of 115-215 from 1985 to 1988. Attendance slipped, and talk of moving the Spurs began.

But luck intervened. In 1987 the Spurs won the NBA draft lottery and picked former U.S. Naval Academy star David Robinson. As a freshman member of the city council, I was part of a delegation that greeted Robinson when he arrived in a private plane at the San Antonio International Airport. The visit was short because he had to fulfill his two-year commitment to the Navy. The Spurs and their fans eagerly awaited his return.

In the meantime Henry Cisneros, who was elected mayor in 1981, was thinking football. San Antonio had shown the nation it could support a major league franchise, and he believed that, with a dome football stadium, it could attract an NFL team. McCombs urged him on, and later it would become clear why he had jumped on board.

In spring 1987 Cisneros turned to Krier, then a state senator, for help establishing a funding mechanism to finance a dome stadium. Although I was a Democrat, I had endorsed Krier, the first Republican I ever supported for public office, when she successfully ran for my old Texas Senate seat in 1984. I encouraged her to push Cisneros's proposed legislation. She teamed up with Sen. Frank Tejeda to introduce legislation that authorized a half-cent temporary sales tax to pay for the dome. The measure would require a public vote to implement.

Cisneros and I, along with an eighty-member delegation, received news that the bill had passed the Senate while we were flying home from Colorado Springs aboard a chartered plane. We had just presented a proposal to host the 1991 Olympic Festival, the largest and most prestigious pre-Olympic event. When Cisneros announced the bill's passage, everyone on the plane cheered.

With only two days left in the session, House passage was problematic. The bill had failed a legislative parliamentary rule that would have permitted House consideration. But in a last-minute maneuver, Rep. Frank Madla led a successful effort to amend a Corpus Christi transit authority bill, adding the provision twenty-five minutes before the session's final gavel. The legislation became known as the "Dracula bill" because it refused to die. After its passage Cisneros launched a massive petition drive to collect signatures to call for the election. Some 2,000 volunteers turned in 76,000 signatures.

In September 1988 I voted, along with the majority of city council, to submit to the voters the opportunity to increase the sales tax by a half-cent for five years to build a dome stadium. The council picked the fifty-five-acre Alamo Iron Works site sandwiched between IH-37 and the Southern Pacific railroad tracks east of downtown. Cisneros kicked off the campaign with a large rally at Villita Assembly Hall with former governor John Connally as the main attraction. Meanwhile the opposition began organizing. The conservative, primarily Anglo Homeowner-Taxpayer Association and the liberal, largely Hispanic, inner-city Communities Organized for Public Service (COPS) joined forces to lead a charge against the proposed tax. The Homeowner-Taxpayer Association was against any new taxes, and COPS was against spending sales tax dollars on sports stadiums. But Cisneros was too strong and too popular. In January 1989 voters approved the sales tax with a 53 percent majority.

When Cisneros decided not to run for reelection, Cockrell, who had preceded him as mayor from 1977 to 1981, was elected to succeed him in May 1989. Soon after, McCombs approached Cockrell about letting the Spurs play in the dome. He complained that the old arena was too small, in bad condition, and unable to accommodate skyboxes. The NBA chimed in, saying the arena was not up to its standards. The city council authorized a study concluding that renovating the arena, without the much-needed skyboxes, would cost more than $40 million.

McCombs had good reason to want to move: NBA basketball was becoming extremely expensive. More seats and skyboxes for corporate clients were necessary to pay for his multimillion-dollar players. Should the city attract a football team, scheduling for basketball and football games in the dome could be worked out, he felt sure.

Cockrell agreed to consider the request. As a councilman, I supported the Spurs' move because I thought the dome would lose money without a football team, and no team was in sight. To be profitable, we needed a strong tenant. In October 1990 we executed a lease with the Spurs that, along with the city's percentage of concessions, would generate approximately $4 million annually, making the dome profitable. After I became mayor in May 1991, building the dome on schedule and under budget became my responsibility.

At the same time, we tried to fulfill Cisneros's dream of an NFL team. McCombs and I made the case for a San Antonio football expansion franchise to the league at its New York headquarters. In March 1992 the NFL announced that San Antonio had not made the short list. Without NFL football, moving the Spurs to the dome proved to be very smart financially for the city.

Soon after the NFL announcement, McCombs told me he had to either sell the Spurs or find additional investors. He said the cost of owning a major sports franchise was prohibitive for a sole owner. For the next year, I worked to find a group of local businesspeople to buy the Spurs. Gen. Robert McDermott, chairman of insurance giant USAA, was the only local chief executive with substantial financial resources to express interest in buying the team. But he needed another major partner, and at the time we did not have one. Then in September 1992 Ed Whitacre Jr., chairman of Southwestern Bell Corp. (SCB), joined Gov. Ann Richards and me in San Antonio to announce that his company would move from St. Louis to our city. In a subsequent meeting with Whitacre, I urged him to partner with McDermott and assemble a local ownership group to buy the Spurs. He agreed to consider it.

I attended the first meeting of a proposed twenty-two-member ownership group at USAA in January 1993. McDermott and Whitacre took the lead, pledging $10 million each. Bartell Zachry, James Leininger, Bill Greehey, Charlie Amato, Tim Hixon, Gary Dudley, Sylvan Stephen Lang, Paul R. Markey, Jeanne Lang Mathews, Bruce and Russell Hill, Dennis Nixon, Felix L. Stehling, and Lowry Mays eventually invested various amounts.

On February 19 I attended a press conference to announce the sale. McDermott was named Spurs chairman, and Bob Coleman was named president. Bob Bass continued as general manager and Russ Bookbinder as vice president of business operations. Later in the year Rick Pych would be hired as vice president and chief financial officer.

I also had to deal with controversies involved in building the dome. The city council adopted a design to suspend the roof from cables attached to four massive corner towers. When we revealed the plans, dome critics jumped on it. Some called it a cattle barn; others, an airplane hangar with four telephones poles; and still others, a dead, upside-down armadillo. Some thought better of it, calling it a third-generation dome and a building of the future. I preferred this view.

Because we were building on an industrial site, we ran into the issue of contaminated dirt. As we sought to address it, some politicians made things worse by exaggerating the problem. Numerous lawsuits were filed against the city. We eventually spent more than $9 million on remediation and removal of dome dirt.

We survived the controversy and opened the Alamodome on May 15, 1993, under budget and on time. We celebrated with an open house for all the citizens of San Antonio. The Alamodome turned out to be an excellent facility with great sight lines, 65,000 comfortable seats, large suites, wide corridors, and a good sound system.

Two months later the Olympic Festival became the dome's first event. By that time Krier, who had led the effort to attract the festival, was Bexar County judge. She joined me in the opening ceremony. In the fall the Spurs played their first game in the dome. The controversy had settled, and citizens seemed pleased with the new landmark—especially after the dome ran in the black its second year and remained there during its first decade.

When McDermott retired from USAA in August 1993, I had concerns about USAA's continued commitment to the Spurs. I knew that the new USAA chairman, Gen. Robert Herres, was not happy about the investment. I also heard about tension in the leadership transition. McDermott continued to be Spurs chairman because he was still a small investor in the team. But because he no longer had the power base of USAA, his prestige was diminished. He no longer carried the clout he had commanded in the previous two decades.

That summer Bass had traded Spurs star Sean Elliott to the Detroit Pistons for rebounding star Dennis Rodman. Rodman had the reputation of a troublemaker, and he immediately did not get along with the other Spurs. Most important, Spurs center David Robinson did not think well of him. In the 1993 playoff series against Utah, Rodman took his shoes off before the first game was over. When Coach John Lucas asked him to put them on and return to the game, he refused. The Spurs lost the series.

McDermott, who was never happy about the Rodman trade, decided it was time for a change in Spurs management. In spring 1994 he led the effort to fire Bass for the botched trade. Coleman supported Bass, and when the board fired him Coleman resigned. The Spurs board then hired Jack Diller as president. A Yale graduate with an extensive sports background, Diller had worked for the New York Mets and New York Knicks. McDermott brought in Gregg Popovich, who had been the assistant coach for the Golden State Warriors, as general manager.

On September 2 McDermott was quoted as saying that the Spurs would commission a feasibility study for a new arena. I was not excited about the idea because the Spurs provided the financial underpinning for the dome's operation. I knew that if the Spurs left, the dome would start losing money.

After the Spurs moved to the Alamodome, the old arena sat mostly vacant. While the dome was under construction, I gained support from both the Texas legislature and the city council to increase the hotel-motel tax to double the size of the convention center. The arena sat in the way of plans for a contiguous expansion of the convention center. I dampened the heat of anger fueled by nostalgia, persuading the city council in January 1994 to raze it. Many Spurs fans shared great memories of their team's nineteen years in the arena. Some never forgave me. But by the time I was term limited out of office in May 1995, the old arena had been demolished.

Meanwhile the Spurs drew large crowds in their new home. Occupying one end of the dome, the Spurs had access to 35,000 seats when they opened the upper deck. That provided many inexpensive seats for important games. But McDermott still was not happy. On July 4, 1995, he called the Alamodome unsuitable for the Spurs. He said the sight lines were bad and the suites, located high in the dome and far from the action, were not suited for watching basketball. Unless they got a new arena, he said, the Spurs might leave San Antonio. Because McDermott's opinions did not carry the weight they once had, Mayor Bill Thornton ignored his threats and hoped the issue would go away.

Spurs president Diller and chief financial officer Pych were aware that the Spurs board needed a strong new leader. Pych later told me: "I'd heard that Peter Holt might be interested. I didn't know him, but I knew Jim Dublin [owner of a public relations firm] was close to him. I asked Jim to call Peter Holt to see if he was interested."

Holt was CEO of Holt Company, one of the largest distributors of the Caterpillar tractor, a machine Holt's grandfather had invented. Over the years our family business had bought several forklifts and front-end loaders from the Holt family. We found them to be fair dealers who kept their word.

In early 1996 Dublin asked me to recommend to Herres that Holt would be a good person to buy USAA's shares of the Spurs. Herres said he was interested and would talk to him.

At the same time, McDermott attempted to sell the Spurs to brothers Joe and Gavin Maloof. Gavin had gone to Trinity University, but both brothers lived in Albuquerque, where, with other family members, they owned a beer distributorship and a regional bank and also ran a casino. They promised to keep the team in San Antonio for at least five years but cautioned that if a new arena had not been built by then, they would have to move the team. The public reacted negatively to the threat, and many angry citizens were ready to let the Spurs move.

While McDermott was negotiating with the Maloof brothers, Holt and his wife, Julianna, bought USAA's 13 percent interest. The board approved the sale in June 1996, and Holt became a board member.

McDermott was out on a limb negotiating a sale that drew skepticism from both the public and the Spurs board of directors. On July 10, after a five-and-a-half-hour board meeting, the Spurs announced that they had rejected the Maloof offer. Embarrassed and hurt by the defeat of his recommendation, McDermott offered his resignation, which was accepted. Holt was elected chairman of the Spurs.

The reaction was immediate. One of the owners, James Leininger, the chief executive officer of Kinetic Concepts, said, "The risk to me [of the Spurs moving] was not acceptable." Holt said, "I didn't buy into the team to sell it less than thirty days later." Thornton said, "I'm glad to see that the deal to sell to owners from Albuquerque wasn't done." Krier said the decision was in the community's best interest, and she believed Holt was a good choice to lead the ownership group.

Later the Holts bought Gaylord Entertainment's 18 percent share and half of SBC's ownership, making them the Spurs' largest shareowner. The team now had a leader who was committed to San Antonio. He was wealthy, aggressive, and charming. He had served in the Army during the Vietnam War, earning a Silver Star, three Bronze Stars, and a Purple Heart. He had the time, talent, and energy to lead the Spurs. And he was ready to take the public stage in San Antonio.

For the sports franchise to convince local officials and the public to build a new sports venue, it needed not only an owner with standing in the community, financial power, and time to devote to the club; it also needed someone to handle external relations. Just two months before Holt was elected chairman, the Spurs had hired Leo Gomez, who had been president of the San Antonio Hispanic Chamber of Commerce, the largest Hispanic chamber in the nation. He became Holt's spokesperson and his link to community leadership. Holt also had the political and legal expertise of Tullos Wells, legal counsel to the Spurs. Wells had been chairman of the Greater San Antonio Chamber of Commerce in 1995.

Holt announced that he wanted to win an NBA championship and build the Spurs a new home. It was time for local officials to pay attention. But the 1996 season got off to a rough start. Starter David Robinson was injured early in the season, and the Spurs began losing. After the first eighteen games, Spurs general manager Gregg Popovich replaced Bob Hill as coach. Without Robinson, the Spurs posted their worst record, a 20–62 win-loss. They were the fourth worst team in the league.

At season's end the NBA conducted its annual weighted lottery. The team with the worst record had the most chances to pick the first choice. As the fourth worst team, the Spurs had a 10 percent chance to win. They hit the jackpot for the second time in their short history, winning the right to pick Wake Forest University star Tim Duncan. Pych later told me, "We were so lucky to win and very fortunate that one of the best college players in many years was eligible for the draft."

With two superstars in Duncan and Robinson, Holt thought the Spurs had a great chance to win an NBA championship. As Popovich began to mold a great team, Holt concentrated on how best to persuade political leaders to build a new arena. To be successful he would need the help of three key elected officials: Judge Krier, Mayor Peak, and Sen. Frank Madla, who had carried the dome financing bill. Holt knew the half-cent sales tax for the dome had expired in 1995. He also knew how hard it would be to persuade voters to renew it; even a strong mayor like Cisneros had garnered only 53 percent of the vote for the original tax.

Holt looked for another way. In spring 1997 he dispatched Gomez to Austin to lobby the Texas legislature. He worked with Madla and Rep. Leticia Van de Putte to develop a bill allowing major urban cities to build sports venues with a combination of taxes, including the hotel-motel tax and sales tax, as well as fees on rental cars, tickets, and parking. The bill required a local public vote to implement.

Van de Putte had to fight numerous amendments on the House floor. One, however, she quietly accepted. That amendment allowed both the county and the city to use the tax. After more than eight and a half hours of debate, the bill passed the House. Madla then passed the bill in the Senate, and Gov. George W. Bush signed it into law.

Years later, over breakfast at Tommy's Courthouse Café, a favorite of city and county politicians, I asked Gomez if the Spurs had supported giving the county the right to use the tax bill. He smiled and said, "The county didn't know it was going to get the authority, but it had two good legislative friends in Austin who took care of it." His remark meant he had whispered in the ears of the legislators to give the county authority.

The next night I was with Van de Putte at the rodeo. "Tell me why you gave the authority to the county to use the tax," I said. She replied: "Because of limited terms and inexperience [on city council]. I didn't think the city would take the long-term view, so I gave the county the right to use the tax as well." That provision should have sent off alarm bells at City Hall. The city had a potential competitor for use of the tax bill. But perhaps city leaders viewed county government, known only for building jails, as ineffective.

After the bill passed, Holt still found no support at City Hall. Peak said he was aware of a poll showing that 80 percent of voters opposed using any tax to pay for an arena. Holt tried another tack. In 1998 he sought to create a tax increment district to build an arena at the Longhorn Quarry near IH-35. Bitterblue Inc., a company owned by Laddie Denton and Gene Powell, controlled the site. In a tax increment district, taxes from the value of any new construction would go to the district to pay off the arena debt. The taxing district needed participation by the North East Independent School District.

Krier was supportive of the Spurs effort because the state would reimburse the school district for any tax funds that went to the arena. The effect was to provide state support for the arena. Peak stayed on the sidelines and did not support the Spurs effort. After a contentious debate in mid-December, the North East school board voted down the Spurs plan. Gomez later told me: "North East Board Chairman Bruce Bennett told me he would support us. He changed his mind right before the meeting and announced he would oppose us. After we lost the vote, all of us, including Peter, were really down."

After the Bitterblue failure, several cities made a play for the Spurs. Baltimore, New Orleans, San Diego, Anaheim, and various ownership groups offered to buy the team. Holt was quoted as saying that the Spurs wanted to stay in San Antonio but needed a new arena.

In 1999 the Spurs began a winning streak. By April it was clear that they would be in the playoffs and had a good chance to win an NBA championship. As the season progressed, Krier called Peak and offered to help with the effort to build a new arena. The two attended a playoff game with Holt, and a good partnership appeared to be in the making. But instead, a battle would break out between the city and county over who would build the arena. Within six months the voters would determine the winner.

The mayor and the county judge had significantly different views about where the arena should be built. Peak wanted it downtown, and Krier preferred the 175-acre Joe and Harry Freeman

Coliseum grounds on the East Side, owned by the county, so that the San Antonio Stock Show & Rodeo and the Spurs could share the facility. While Krier continued to talk with Peak, she asked county staff to plan how the county could build an arena. She also talked with Jack Rains, who had led Houston's effort to build a sports facility.

In the meantime Holt commissioned a poll from Baselice and Associates. The results of the April 18–21 polling showed that 88 percent of voters had heard about the possibility of building a new arena. Unfortunately 50 percent said they were less likely to support building a new arena, and 64 percent said they were predisposed to vote against a half-cent sales tax to pay for it. Although the sales tax to pay for the dome had expired in 1994, 28 percent thought it was still in effect and 27 percent were not sure. Only 20 percent believed a new arena should be built next to the Alamodome, while 43 percent favored the coliseum grounds.

The 1998–99 basketball season was shortened to fifty games because the league locked out the players to force a new collective bargaining agreement, finally reached in January. But magic struck in the playoffs. With just twelve seconds left in the Western Conference finals against the Portland Trail Blazers, Sean Elliott sank a three-pointer to overcome a two-point deficit. The "Memorial Day Miracle" helped propel the Spurs into the NBA finals. As you may recall, this was the same Elliott who had been traded away in 1993. The next year he was brought back, and Rodman was dispatched to the Chicago Bulls. Robinson and Duncan went on to lead the Spurs to victory over the New York Knicks in the NBA finals. On June 25 the Spurs won the championship, and the city went crazy. Duncan was named the finals MVP. More than 300,000 citizens showed up at a river parade to celebrate the victory. Peak and Krier rode on one of the river floats as fans chanted, "Arena, arena, arena."

Holt knew that sports victories fade as do sports stars. He needed the glow of victory, so he pushed for a vote to build a new arena on November 2, only four months after the championship run. Although Peak had downplayed the need for a new arena right up to the championship, he immediately thereafter announced that he wanted to make a real effort to build one.

Later Peak told me over lunch at the Houston Street Bistro, "After the Spurs won the championship, Alex [City Manager Alex Briseño] and I met with Peter Holt and other Spurs officials at Bob Coleman's office." Coleman, onetime Spurs president, had been a longtime leader of the San Antonio Sports Foundation and was a former minority investor in the Spurs. "Peter said the Spurs would stick with us as long as I supported building a new arena and the city actually moved forward," Peak continued. "I agreed and said I would direct staff to come up with a proposal using the sales tax. After that meeting, I never thought the Spurs would consider any county proposal."

When I asked Gomez about that first meeting he said: "We told Mayor Peak that our polls showed we would lose a sales tax vote even though we had won the championship. We told him the hotel-motel tax would pass. I still don't understand why he refused to use the hotel-motel tax."

I called Peak for his response and he said: "I told the Spurs I wouldn't consider using the hotel-motel tax because I felt any increase in the tax would hurt tourism. As mayor, you had just passed a large increase to build the new convention center. An additional increase would make us the highest in the state. If we ever needed to increase the hotel-motel tax in the future, it should go to finance future expansion of the city's convention facilities."

I understood his position. The hotel-motel industry and the city worked closely together in promoting tourism and managing convention facilities. A commission made up mostly of tourism industry officials oversees the city's operation. The hotel-motel industry did not support raising the hotel-motel tax to pay for an arena. Its members thought a new arena would not bring more overnight visitors to San Antonio. Peak was not about to take an action that he viewed as stabbing his partner in the back.

But Holt was leery of the sales tax idea. He knew the county had no ties to the hotel-motel industry and that Krier would consider using the hotel-motel tax. He also appreciated Krier's efforts to build a new arena using a tax increment district with North East Independent School District. With her support, he had a reserve plan.

Just a few days after winning the championship, Holt hosted a two-hour joint meeting with Peak and Krier. City and county staff also attended. Peak later told me: "I told the Spurs I wanted to protect the public investment in the dome by building the arena on the south parking lot of the Alamodome, connecting the two facilities by an underground tunnel. I proposed that the two facilities should be both managed by the city. I said downtown offered a better venue for sports fans because restaurants, retail, and hotels were within walking distance. I told the Spurs we could pass the sales tax."

Later I had lunch with Krier at The Palm on Houston Street. The restaurant features drawings of local civic leaders on its walls. Along with Houston Street Bistro it has become a favorite gathering place for downtown businesspeople and professionals. She told me: "I proposed that we create a city-county commission to study where the arena should be built and how it would be financed. I said a city-county sports authority could be formed to build the arena and then jointly operate the coliseum, dome, and arena. I said if the arena were built on the coliseum grounds, both facilities could be jointly operated. After all, I was a supporter of building the Alamodome. I didn't want it to fail. I also knew the prospectus for operating the dome did not include the Spurs playing in the dome. Voters had approved the dome without any plans for the Spurs to play there."

Peak was not in the mood for compromise. One week after the meeting with Krier and Holt, he announced that he would not agree to form a joint committee with the county, nor would he agree to any report that said the arena should be built on coliseum grounds. The city and county should continue to work on their own plans, he said, and once the Spurs decided which plan to accept, the city and county should work in unison to see how each one could help the other.

City Manager Briseño backed Peak. In a speech to the San Antonio Area Tourism Council he said it would be very difficult for the public to comprehend raising the hotel-motel tax. He also said the arena should be located downtown by the dome. But Krier had not let any grass grow under her feet. By the time Peak announced that the city and county should go their separate ways, she had a preliminary plan. On July 12 county staff, under the leadership of David Morgan, information services director, and Marcus Jahns, budget director, presented an eight-page Freeman Coliseum arena project planning outline. The unsightly area housed a collection of barns behind the more than half-century-old coliseum. The only major event that occurred on the site was the annual rodeo.

While this epic battle was heating up I was running our family business, Sun Harvest, a nine-store chain of natural supermarkets. I had followed the debate, urging Peak and Krier to find common ground. I wrote Peak a letter on July 12 stating: "It makes sense, then, to build the arena on the south end of the dome and connect the two by a passageway. This would enable one management team to run both facilities. If, for some reason, the arena cannot be built on the south of the dome and is built, instead, on the coliseum site, then the dome and arena should be managed by one entity."

The *San Antonio Express-News* Editorial Board entered the battle on Peak's side. The newspaper wrote that the arena should be located downtown and paid for with sales tax proceeds. It advocated that the Spurs play some games in the dome to allow thousands of low-income fans to attend. Krier later told me: "I tried to persuade the Spurs to play some of their games in the dome. I believe they tried, but city attitudes and the complication of season tickets doomed the effort. When that effort failed, we put requirements for low-cost tickets in the new arena into the contract."

Peak and Briseño both thought they held all the face cards. They knew they were the big boys of local government and believed their opponent did not have the firepower. Bexar County had never been a major player in economic development initiatives. They also thought Commissioners Court would have a hard time gaining consensus within its own shop. The court had to work with an independent five-member Coliseum Advisory Board they appointed as landlord of the 175-acre grounds; they also had to work with the San Antonio Livestock Exposition, or SALE. The three entities had a history of fighting about concessions, rent, and facilities maintenance. Now the Spurs would be thrown into the mix. The city did not think cowboys, basketball players, and county politicians could join forces to move the Spurs to a county facility.

The San Antonio Stock Show & Rodeo had a much longer history in the city than did the Spurs. The area ranching industry began around 1750. Spanish settlers grew maize and raised cattle, launching what became our principal industry. The vaqueros of Spain and then Mexico founded the ranches where each year they rounded up and branded their cattle, a process called a rodeo. During the roundup, the vaqueros enjoyed testing their roping and riding skills.

The era of the cowboy reached its height after the Civil War when vaqueros and cowboys organized trail rides, driving cattle from South Texas to as far north as Montana. San Antonio became a major intersection for the famous Chisholm Trail and other trails, according to Frank Jennings in his book *San Antonio: The Story of an Enchanted City*. But the era was short-lived as trains emerged to provide stock cars and as barbed wire destroyed the open range in the 1880s.

Cowboys continued to work on ranches, but they sought more than the hard work of mending fences and caring for cattle. In 1936 they formed the Professional Rodeo Cowboys Association, which staged events across the nation such as bareback riding, calf roping, bull riding, steer wrestling, and saddle bronc riding. The association set up headquarters in Colorado Springs, with the ProRodeo Hall of Fame and the Museum of the American Cowboy next door.

The rodeo grew in popularity over the years, as did livestock shows, which exhibited and judged farm animals. Future Farmers of America and 4-H clubs were created to encourage youth to care for and show pigs, horses, sheep, goats, and cattle. The shows fostered a better understanding of how to raise livestock and improve meat quality.

San Antonio lacked a proper facility to hold a rodeo and livestock show. In 1948 Joe Freeman led an effort to build a multipurpose coliseum on county property to be used for a stock show and rodeo. On February 17, 1950, the first San Antonio Stock Show & Rodeo took place, with a mission to "support youth today so that agriculture can grow tomorrow." More than 250,000 people attended the event in the following two weeks.

Over the years the rodeo outgrew the coliseum. In the seven years previous, the rodeo had sold out every performance. Mary Nan West, longtime chair of SALE, had a history of controlling the coliseum grounds. She often lived in a trailer on the grounds despite owning a multimillion-dollar ranch south of town. She also had a history of liking the status quo. Other than some new barns, no major improvements had been made to the grounds since the coliseum had been built some fifty years earlier. When, as mayor, I advocated building a baseball park on coliseum grounds, West rebuffed me. She had no enthusiasm for Krier's efforts to schedule hockey teams, sales events, and other revenue generators in the coliseum. I must admit that, at the time, I thought Peak was right. The county would never get its act together.

But the county had some hidden face cards. Commissioners Court had strengthened the county's management team when it hired Jahns as budget director in 1993. Five years later the court hired David Morgan as information services director. He had previously been executive director for the Dallas Downtown Sports Development Project, where for three years he worked on building an arena for the Dallas Mavericks. Morgan pulled together some consultants he had used to build the Mavericks' arena.

The county had a popular, experienced district attorney in Susan Reed. Her office had a staff of fifteen civil attorneys that represented Commissioners Court. Her chief civil attorney, Ed Schweninger, and Krier's chief of staff, Seth Mitchell, led the county team over many hurdles. The county also had the more popular tax to propose; it is always easier to tax a visitor than a resident—in this case, tourists who stayed in hotels and rented cars. The experienced county commissioners supported the hotel-motel and car rental taxes while their counterparts at City Hall kept barking up the sales tax tree. The county also had the rodeo folks on its side. SALE had thousands of supporters who would provide a major grassroots political force to pass the initiative.

The *Express-News* published a poll conducted by the University of Texas at San Antonio showing that 60 percent of people would not approve an arena built with taxpayer dollars. But 64 percent said it was important to keep the Spurs in town. The Spurs did a little polling of their own that summer, which revealed that voters would support an increase in the hotel-motel tax but not an increase in the sales tax. The poll also indicated that the voters preferred the coliseum site to downtown.

COPS and Metro Alliance, two powerful inner-city activist organizations, told Peak they would not support a sales tax initiative for the arena. Instead they wanted to vote on a sales tax in November to pay for a human development fund for job training and education.

Meanwhile the county moved forward to get their house in order. Banker Tom Frost, a great supporter of SALE, agreed to host a meeting between Holt and SALE officials West, Norm Nevins, and Keith Martin. When Holt told West the exposition could have exclusive control of the arena during the rodeo, she warmed to the plan. She realized the arena would take the rodeo to a new level, and it was too good a deal to pass up.

Once again Commissioners Court held out a hand to the city. On July 27 they voted unanimously to invite the city to participate in a city-county joint sports authority. But there were no takers. The city intended to win the battle.

Brushed aside by the city, Commissioners Court continued to work with the Spurs to develop a county plan calling for a public-private venture. The hotel-motel and car rental taxes would pay for $146 million of the construction, and the Spurs would contribute an additional $28.5 million. The Spurs would be responsible for building the arena and covering all construction cost overruns. They would pay an annual rental fee of $1.3 million toward debt reduction under a twenty-five-year lease. They would negotiate naming rights and receive all revenue from parking, advertising, and arena rental. They would also manage the arena and assume responsibility for any operational loses. The county would receive some naming rights revenue and profit sharing from the arena above certain thresholds. For a three-week period during the rodeo, SALE would control the arena.

Krier later told me: "When I first ran for county judge in 1992, one of the commitments I made was to improve the facilities for the rodeo. The coliseum was in bad shape, and other interests were always trying to lure the rodeo away. I now had the opportunity to provide a needed facility for the Stock Show & Rodeo, the Spurs, and several other events. My main focus was on not making money for the county on the arena, but rather on not losing money. I didn't want the county to be responsible for cost overruns on building the arena or for any operational deficits."

After the county proposal became public, I met with Peak and urged him to give the Spurs a firm offer and set a short acceptance deadline. I told him that the longer the Spurs played the city against the county, the more concessions they would get from the county. The next day the *Express-News* carried some of my comments. It wrote: "Wolff says, 'The Spurs need to get off center and choose who they are going with. They have had a profitable and long relationship with the city, and they should stick with their partner.' "

On July 28 city staff recommended to the council that a one-eighth-cent sales tax be levied for twenty-one years to build a $203 million arena and parking garage next to the Alamodome. The staff also recommended submitting three other issues to the voters: a one-eighth-cent sales tax for better jobs, a one-eighth-cent sales tax for citywide economic development facilities, and a one-eighth-cent sales tax for economic development projects for each council district.

Peak set an August 12 deadline to conclude negotiations with the Spurs. He picked this date because the deadline for submitting an election plan to the Justice Department was one week later. Unfortunately for the city Peak's deadline gave the Spurs enough time to reach an agreement with the county.

While the Spurs, led by Pych, continued to negotiate with the county, the city changed its offer, proposing a quarter-cent sales tax for ten years to pay for the construction. It wanted the Spurs to sign a twenty-year lease and build the arena for a guaranteed maximum price. The city would own, operate, and maintain the arena and have use of it for all dates other than Spurs games. The Spurs would pay $1.5 million in rent. In addition the city would get 100 percent of concession revenue above the Spurs' 40 percent concession fee. The city would participate financially in naming rights and receive compensation for a portion of suite food and beverage, ticket sales, a facility fee, and parking.

As the terms of the two deals became public, it was clear which deal was better for the Spurs. The county gave up naming rights, concessions, parking, and ticket sales. It also gave the Spurs full control of the arena except during the rodeo for the same rent that the city would charge for just the Spurs games. The city was negotiating as if it did not have competition.

On August 2 Peak and I advocated the downtown arena on a show taped at KSAT-TV studios, the local ABC affiliate. Afterward he said to me, "The Spurs are going to call a press conference this Thursday to announce that they're going with the city. Judge Krier is going to join us." I congratulated him and added, "I didn't think you could pull it off after I saw the two proposals."

Two days later Krier and Peak met and shared their plans. On the same day, a watchdog group calling itself Citizens Alliance for Better Government threatened to recall three or four council members if they set a November vote to pay for the arena with a sales tax.

The next day the city council met in executive session. After the meeting Peak said, "We haven't struck a deal formally, but we're coming closer." Later that day the council held a public hearing at which eighty people spoke. Leading the opposition was Father Walter D'heedene, a spokesman for COPS-Metro Alliance. He said, "You're asking the working poor people of San Antonio to give of their most precious belongings to build your golden calf." Arthur Emerson, chairman of the Greater San Antonio Chamber of Commerce, spoke in favor of the sales tax plan.

Four days later at a press conference, Father D'heedene and Andy Sarabia, another COPS-Metro leader, announced that the groups supported the county plan. They said an increase in the hotel-motel tax would not hurt low-income and middle-income taxpayers. Krier was there to thank them for their support. Instead of using the Bexar County Courthouse for their announcement, they chose the steps of City Hall to poke Peak in the eye. That had to hurt.

Krier later told me: "I had the support of both bookends of the local political spectrum. The conservative Homeowner-Taxpayer Association and the liberal COPS-Metro Alliance supported the county plan over the city's sales tax approach."

The following day Peak wrote Krier a letter outlining fourteen questions about the county's proposal. He concluded by saying these were only a few of the questions. The next morning, at a Spurs board meeting, Holt presented a new Baselice and Associates poll conducted August 5–8. Results showed that voters favored the county's proposal over the city's, 49 percent to 23 percent. Among those polled, 47 percent said they would vote for the hotel-motel and car rental tax while 45 percent would vote against it. The county's approach was clearly a winnable campaign. After a long discussion, the board voted for the plan. The only opposing board member was Bill Greehey, chairman of Valero Energy Co. He believed the Spurs should stick with the city and build downtown. Later that day Holt held a press conference at the courthouse with Krier and Commissioners Court. He said the determining factor was the poll showing strong opposition to a sales tax increase.

Peak was quoted the next day as saying, "My understanding is they're [the county] essentially turning everything over to the Spurs." Briseño was quoted as saying, "I do think that he [Mayor Peak] got hung out by the Spurs. Overall, I think it's going to be a loss for the community." The Hotel-Motel Association immediately announced that it would oppose the tax and would raise $500,000 to fight the referendum. Doug Beach, chairman of the Tourism Council, released a survey showing that 77 percent of respondents said they would not plan meetings in San Antonio if the tax increased again.

The Spurs were ready to do battle. They organized the Saddle and Spurs campaign, mixing cowboys and basketball players. They named Hope Andrade the treasurer. Public Strategies' Eddie Alderete ran the campaign. Later Alderete said to me: "I've never been in a campaign where money was not a problem. Peter would say, 'Are you sure we're spending enough?' I believe we ended up spending about $2.8 million. Over $1 million was spent on television, radio, and direct mail. We delivered voter registration kits to new potential voters, provided transportation to the polls, and kept up a strong phone bank calling voters."

As the campaign got under way, Peak composed another letter to Krier on August 17: "It would be a travesty of public policy to support a program that would redirect revenues currently generated by these public investments [Alamodome and tourism] into largely private hands [the Spurs]." He added that he would withhold support for the county plan until the fourteen questions outlined in his August 10 letter had been answered.

Krier gave Peak a ten-page response. Even though the Spurs had selected the county plan, she again invited the city to create a joint city-county sports and entertainment authority to co-manage the proposed arena, which would be located next to the coliseum. "It can ensure that we do not underbid each other on events," she wrote, "and that local marketing efforts are more coordinated, more cost-effective, and more successful."

At lunch with Holt on August 18, I said: "You know I supported the city, but that battle is over. I'm going to support the campaign, but I hope you'll try to repair the damage with Mayor Peak by working out a joint marketing arrangement with the dome." Holt said he'd met with the mayor at Spurs partner Charlie Amato's office earlier that day and that they would work on a joint marketing plan. "Great," I said. "I look forward to helping on the campaign."

The lead negotiators for the Spurs, the county, SALE, and the Coliseum Advisory Board met all day on August 21. They debated six versions of the letter of intent before reaching a general agreement. Three days later Commissioners Court approved the letter and set the election for November 2.

A few days later I attended a public meeting hosted by the San Antonio Greater Chamber of Commerce at Incarnate Word College (now University of the Incarnate Word). Mary Nan West stole the show with a rousing speech supporting the agreement. She delivered a six-word speech that became a campaign mantra: "More seats, more money, more scholarships." Her backing was huge because SALE had thousands of supporters. Jackie Van De Walle-Dreher took on the task of organizing campaign volunteers. The cowboys were dribbling faster than their partner, the Spurs; Holt, a rancher, loved it. The Tourism Council declined to attend the chamber event; they thought it unfair that the chamber did not give the city a chance to express its views.

That same day a key leader of the tourism industry, Bill Lyons, owner of the venerable restaurant Casa Rio, sent the chamber board a letter opposing the hotel-motel tax. "A vital downtown and tourism industry is more important to the future of our community and its citizens than either the Spurs or their arena," he wrote.

When an *Express-News* reporter asked my views on the tax, I said I did not think the increase would be as devastating as the association contended. I based my views on a study by consulting firm Texas Perspectives, which found that raising the tax would result in a slightly slower rate of expected revenue growth, but that the arena project would offset that with increased tourism activity.

Following up on our lunch conversation, Holt wrote Peak a letter offering to create a joint marketing effort. The Spurs proposed selling suites and signs for both the arena and the dome if they received the concession rights. In turn, the Spurs would guarantee the city an annual payment of $250,000, as well as 50 percent of all revenue in excess of $500,000 annually.

On September 7 a television spot promoting the initiative hit the airwaves, the first of many to come. As the campaign progressed, Peak stayed on the sidelines. I called to tell him the Greater Chamber would soon vote on whether to support the Spurs campaign and I would speak in support. I had served as chair of the chamber the year before and was still a board member. I asked him if he wanted to make a statement before the vote, and he said, "I'll write a letter to Arthur Emerson [chamber chair]." Peak wrote

Emerson that the Spurs move would have a $2 million negative impact on the dome and that the increased motel-hotel tax would hurt the tourism industry and jeopardize future expansion of the convention center. He said the city would not pay for city streets and drainage improvements needed near the coliseum grounds.

On September 30 I urged the Greater Chamber board to support building the arena. The board voted in favor, with the provision that a joint marketing and management agreement be developed for the Alamodome and the arena. The city never did accept the joint marketing agreement Holt offered.

Meanwhile the Spurs and the county were growing testy with each other. While they had a letter of intent, they had no binding agreement. There were disagreements over revenue sharing, rent, and length of the lease. Krier later told me: "I was at the kickoff of the United Way campaign with Peter Holt. I was very frustrated with the arena negotiations. I asked him to meet me upstairs in his office. While I was in the Senate, he had given me a book titled *Getting to Yes*. It was a book about how to manage by principles. I threw it on his desk and told him he should reread it. He said the book was hogwash. After that, my belief that we could negotiate on what was in the best interest of the community vanished. I knew that I had to do what was best for the county, and he would do what was best for the Spurs."

I had lunch with Tullos Wells at Club Giraud, a private club on the grounds of the former Ursuline Convent and Academy. He told me: "The negotiations were really rough. Peter got into it with Joe Bradbury [chairman of the Coliseum Advisory Board] at one of the sessions in my office. Peter was in a rip-roaring, snorting snit. He yelled at Bradbury, saying the county was dealing him death by a thousand slices."

In an October 4 letter to Krier and the commissioners, Holt wrote: "These past two months of meetings and negotiations have indicated that the process for reaching a multi-party agreement to achieve the project has become extremely difficult. . . . I have executed two different binding agreements." One of the binding agreements provided for the Spurs to develop, operate, and manage the arena, which was consistent with the letter of intent. The other provided for the Spurs to build the arena and the county to operate it. Krier later told me, "One night during the negotiations we [the commissioners, which included Paul Elizondo, Robert Tejeda, Lyle Larson, and Tommy Adkisson] stayed at the courthouse all night long working on the agreements."

While the county was trying to reach an agreement with the Spurs, the opposition brought in Joanna Cagan, author of the book *Field of Schemes*. At a press conference she described the Spurs investment of $28 million in the arena as a pittance. She said stadiums financed in the last ten years averaged a 43 percent investment by the private sector. The Spurs' investment was only 16 percent. But she ignored the important bottom-line agreements that capped taxpayer contributions and made the Spurs responsible for all construction and operational cost overruns.

Finally, on October 12 all parties approved the memorandum of agreement with the Spurs to build and operate the arena. Early voting for the arena election began four days later.

Gene Powell, a big campaign supporter of Peak, wrote him a memo. He copied me, writing at the top of memorandum: "Nelson,

I know you told me that I am barking up a dead tree—but I am not willing to give Howard a pass on this one!" To Peak he wrote: "The political influence inherent in your office is of little use to the community if you keep that influence under a basket. . . . A victory on Tuesday will continue that line of difficult, but correct decisions. A defeat on Tuesday will truly harm and damage our city."

Peak never offered his support to the campaign.

In the meantime the Saddle and Spurs campaign was in full swing. Campaign manager Eddie Alderete later told me: "This was the best-organized campaign I've ever been involved in. We had a strategy session every Monday morning. Judge Krier, Tom Frost, Jackie Van De Walle-Dreher, Jim Lunz, and Peter Holt attended most or all the meetings. We spent a lot of money on polling to make sure our message was on target. Commissioner Adkisson worked very hard on the grassroots campaign."

I asked, "What voters did you target? He answered, "Our strongest Spurs supporters were young Hispanic males living in the inner city and making less than $50,000 a year. We made a major effort to get them to the polls. We knew they would vote with us." As for the rest of the voters, Alderete said, "We knew the most consistent voter would be North Side Anglos over forty-five years old who own a home and make over $50,000. We ran ads that focused on the rodeo, the Shrine circus, and other events we knew they would relate to."

Krier was instrumental in developing this strategy. She had found a fifty-year-old newspaper ad from the campaign to build the coliseum. It promoted using the facility for rodeos, track meets, garden shows, and aircraft displays. She felt what worked then would work now. The Spurs kept up their television barrage featuring Spurs All-Star Sean Elliott, Krier, boxer Jesse James Leija, and banker and SALE officer Tom Frost. They also ran ads assuring people that no sales tax or property tax would be used.

Adkisson played an important role at the grassroots level. He later told me: "I became inspired about the campaign when I saw a car in front of me that had a slogan painted with shoe polish on the back window. It read, 'S.A. Spurs, we will always remember you.' I realized this person was living vicariously through the Spurs. The Spurs' success represented that person's aspirations and dreams for a greater San Antonio."

On election night the Spurs were playing the Philadelphia 76ers in the Alamodome. David Stern, the NBA commissioner, gave out the championship rings and unveiled the championship banner that day. It made for a nice backdrop on election day.

Krier watched the returns with campaign workers in the lamb barn on the coliseum grounds. She later told me, "When the early returns came in, I knew we would win." She was right. The voters overwhelmingly authorized the tax increase by a vote of 113,583 to 71,788. Of 599 voting precincts, only 45 went against the arena. Holt joined campaign workers after the Spurs crowd had been told of the victory. Krier said: "It was an exciting night, but I knew it was just the beginning. Now we had to build the arena and fulfill all our promises."

This was a great victory for Krier, who had taken the lead in securing a new home for the Spurs and the rodeo. In addition she had enhanced the clout of county government. No longer could people easily dismiss the county as a second-rate governmental entity. A new era would begin with Bexar County as an equal partner with the city on many development projects. Krier had outmaneuvered Peak, and the politically inexperienced city council members never knew what hit them.

When Peak, by then a former mayor, and I had lunch in June 2004 at the Houston Street Bistro, he was still smarting from the arena battle. "It was a mistake to build the arena on the East Side," he said. "It should be downtown. We could have passed the sales tax. It was wrong to use the hotel-motel tax. The Spurs misled me in the negotiations."

But as Yogi Berra said, "It ain't over till it's over." Numerous agreements were required to define what kind of building would be built. Krier asked Commissioners Elizondo and Larson to lead the negotiations. Pych was the Spurs' lead negotiator. Negotiations dragged on through the first half of 2000, until Holt again expressed his anger. On June 12 he wrote a letter stating that he would not negotiate further and that if the contracts were not approved by the following Friday, the deal was off. He then later quietly agreed to compromise on the remaining sticking points.

On June 16 Commissioners Court and the Coliseum Advisory Board jointly signed six contracts with the Spurs that specified how the Spurs would operate, design, and build the $175 million facility. In July Ed Whitacre Jr., after leading the local effort to purchase the Spurs in 1993, pledged $41 million over a period of years for naming rights for the company he led, SBC.

On August 23 I attended the groundbreaking for the new arena. When I asked District Attorney Susan Reed where Krier was, she replied, "She's not here." When I asked her husband, Joe

Krier, about it, he said, "There was a misunderstanding regarding the groundbreaking date. She had another commitment." Groundbreakings for major public buildings are symbolically important for a community. Without her leadership, there would have been no arena. The groundbreaking should have been whenever she wanted it. She later told me: "It was just fluff. No big deal. I didn't need to be reinforced. Let them have the glory."

Krier served as Bexar County judge from 1992 to May 2001. She was the first woman and first Republican to hold that office. When she was first elected, I was mayor and we had a great working relationship. As a private citizen, I assisted her efforts to pass the arena initiative. Her husband, who is president of the Greater Chamber, and I are also good friends. Because of our longstanding friendship and working history, Krier supported my appointment to succeed her as county judge—even though I am a Democrat. She believes in bipartisanship as much as I do. I have since successfully run for reelection twice.

Krier left the county a great legacy. I have tried to build on that legacy by thrusting Bexar County into leadership positions on many other important economic projects. In fact, my first job was to oversee the arena's completion. When I became judge, all that existed was a deep hole in the ground. Workers had begun pouring concrete for the foundation. I was in a position similar to the one I had been in when I became mayor in 1991. My responsibility then was to see that the dome got built; now my job was to oversee construction of the arena.

When I was mayor, the city council was responsible for all contracts regarding the Alamodome. We had to buy the site and hire the architects, engineers, and general contractor. We had to approve all the plans. City staff, headed by Roland Lozano, directed the day-to-day construction. Any mistakes landed at my doorstep. When work on the dome was finished, we assumed responsibility for operating it. As I stated earlier, it was a traumatic time.

But my relationship to the arena was different. Under the contract, the county's responsibility was to make sure the Spurs built the arena according to specifications. We had no operational responsibilities. As construction progressed, I enjoyed visiting the site numerous times. Commissioners Court's task was to make sure the Spurs corrected any problems. The Spurs always responded to our concerns and did a great job. In fact, they exceeded the minority contracting provisions, going beyond 32 percent participation. The project went over budget, but under the agreement the Spurs picked up the additional cost.

As completion neared, bookings for the arena began to fill. In September 2002 we held a joint press conference with the Spurs to announce numerous events. John Montford, SBC senior vice president; Holt; Bradbury; and I cut a cake modeled after the arena. I made a few remarks praising my predecessor, Krier, and the court that served with her.

We had a ribbon-cutting ceremony on October 18 to celebrate the arena's opening. For the first time, citizens could see the inside of this first-class structure. While the outside looked like so many other arenas, the inside was unique. Julianna Holt displayed excellent taste in selecting materials and colors. She also led the effort to purchase more than $1 million in art. Consultant Alice Carrington selected twenty-five local artists to create unique pieces. Inside the entrance, a ninety-foot-wide mural by Charles Ingram traces the area's roots from the Spanish conquistadors to the modern era. Anchored to the ceiling is a thirty-one-foot-long, neon-lit *Atomic Spur* designed by George Cisneros. Numerous other artworks are located throughout the arena. The colors and textures of the walls and floors, punctuated by the art, give the arena a warm and welcoming feeling. Julianna Holt deserves the credit for creating a one-of-a-kind sports arena.

On October 27, a week after the ribbon-cutting and, by chance, my birthday, we opened the SBC Center—which later became the AT&T Center when SBC acquired AT&T—for a day of family activities. We held a grand opening on November 1, the night of the Spurs' first regular season game.

All of the city's major political players touched by the arena and dome battles emerged scarred to some extent. Cisneros is now the CEO of American Sunrise. He still gets blamed for the Alamodome's perceived failure. Peak, currently an AT&T executive, still has hard feelings over losing the Spurs to the county. Krier is an attorney for USAA. She told me that while she remains a Spurs fan, she doesn't attend games as often because they are not as much fun after the arena saga. Cockrell, the executive director of the San Antonio Parks Foundation, faired best with no more than a scratch. For fans of the old arena, I am still vilified for taking it down.

TWO

· ·

The PGA Village

TIGHTLY LIMITED TERMS FOR San Antonio's mayor and city council members offer one real advantage to an outgoing mayor. He or she can pass off to his or her successor a highly controversial issue that he or she initiated but did not complete, leaving behind the nasty, contentious debate it generates. One of the most difficult handoffs was the proposal to develop an upscale golf resort called the PGA Village.

In February 2001 Lumbermen's Investment Corp. and the PGA of America (Professional Golfer's Association) announced plans to build a thirty-six-hole golf resort off U.S. 281 at Bulverde and Evans roads. The proposed development would be over a sensitive area of the recharge zone where water drains into the Edwards Aquifer, the source of water for San Antonio and surrounding areas.

Lumbermen's Investment, a division of the Fortune 500 company Temple-Inland, owned the 2,855-acre tract. Adjacent to two golf courses, Lumbermen's planned to build a resort hotel, 4,000 homes, apartments and condos, and other commercial projects. But to make the project work, Lumbermen's needed a little help from the Texas legislature. The company wanted the legislature to create a taxing district that it would control, to be called the Cibolo Canyon Conservation and Improvement District No. 1.

This was unlike any other taxing district in Texas. In fact, it was more like a city. The legislation would give the district the power to impose ad valorem, sales, and use taxes; hotel occupancy taxes; assessments; and impact fees. It also would have the power to employ security, regulate the use of streets and public spaces, and exercise eminent domain within its boundaries. The initial members of the district's board were determined by the legislation. They would be responsible for taxing and spending the proceeds within the district.

The legislation did include one safeguard: a development agreement had to be reached with the City of San Antonio before the district could take effect. Though this provision was helpful, there was great concern that the developers and their astute lawyers would outgun the city in crafting a development agreement. As my friend Pat Maloney, the late trial attorney, told me, "The problem in reaching an agreement with the developers is that they lie so much." If the taxpayers and the environment were to be protected, the city council would have to drive a very tough bargain.

Lumbermen's strong political connections in the legislature paved the way for quick passage. The city's support gave political cover for Lumbermen's. The legislation passed on March 8, 2001, during the waning days of Mayor Howard Peak's second term. The mayoral campaign to succeed Peak was in full swing when the legislation passed, but the PGA development was not a major issue.

Lumbermen's hired a City Hall insider, attorney Bill Kaufman, as its lobbyist. He quickly gathered six council votes, a majority.

But he did not have the mayor's vote. Garza held his cards close to his vest, and thus city staff followed the direction of the council majority.

As much as Garza might have wished to avoid this controversy, the day of reckoning would arrive. The longer he delayed, the more difficult that day would become. In the meantime, his hands-off approach left a leadership vacuum on the council. With six council votes, Lumbermen's began spreading the word that it did not matter how the mayor voted. The developer began to push for an early vote. Garza's delays also gave time for opposition to form. By fall 2001 various environmental organizations, led by architect David Lake, began to mobilize against the development agreement. COPS-Metro Alliance became a partner in the Smart Growth Coalition.

Why was the PGA development such a divisive issue? The confrontation with environmental groups against developers replayed battles about development over the aquifer recharge zone. Aquifer protection has a history of emotional and vitriolic fights. For most of its history, San Antonio has been the largest U.S. city without a surface water supply. The Edwards Aquifer, a porous karst limestone formation stretching 185 miles across six counties, has been the city's major water source. Most water flowing into the aquifer comes from rivers and streams crossing it in Uvalde and Medina counties west of San Antonio. Some rainwater also flows directly into the aquifer.

The aquifer recharges rapidly, and water flows through it quickly—moving from the west, passing through Bexar County, and exiting east of the city at springs in Comal and Hays counties. About 6 percent of the recharge enters the aquifer through crevices and sinkholes in north Bexar County. Although the north band of the recharge zone provides only 6 percent of the recharge, that area presents the greatest threat for pollutants to enter the aquifer because that is where most development over the recharge zone occurs. And that is where the PGA Village was proposed.

Since the 1970s citizen groups have tried to stop development over the recharge zone. In 1975 voters passed a referendum over-ruling a city council decision allowing a mall to be built on the recharge zone. A court later held that the referendum was uncon-stitutional. After that failure, the city funded a study to determine sensitive areas of the recharge zone and make recommendations to protect them. But for years the study gathered dust on a shelf.

Twelve years after the mall battle, in 1987, Mayor Henry Cisneros reignited the flame. In April, one month before I was elected to the city council, Cisneros was on the losing side of an 8-2 zoning vote that allowed a mall to be built over the recharge zone, at the corner of Northwest Military Drive and Loop 1604. Defending his position, he said he was opposed to large-scale development over the zone, which could pose a threat to the city's water supply. For other reasons, the mall was never built.

In May Cisneros held an aquifer recharge protection hear-ing at McAllister Auditorium; more than 1,000 people attended. Tensions ran high as several speakers called for protection mea-sures. Members of the business community responded that such regulations were unnecessary because no study had found that existing development had polluted the aquifer.

After the hearing Cisneros appointed me to a five-member council committee to create recommendations to protect the recharge zone. Four months after our first meeting, our committee issued a report with twenty-nine major recommendations, including stricter standards for sewer lines, limits on septic tanks, and a ban on certain businesses next to sensitive recharge features. Over the next few years the city council implemented most of these recommendations.

After I was elected mayor in 1991, development over the recharge zone began to accelerate, leading me to believe that we needed additional protection measures. In 1994 I appointed environmentalist Danielle Milam and engineer Gene Dawson to head a task force recommending additional development restrictions over the recharge zone. Debate within the task force was unending, and the group was unable to reach a consensus. I hired Jim Blackburn, a Houston environmental attorney who had represented the Audubon Society in preserving wetlands near Houston, to help the task force reach a decision. To give the group time to reach an agreement, on September 14 the city council passed a moratorium on development over the recharge zone. Finally the task force agreed to a twenty-nine-page document imposing new regulations. In an action hailed as a major victory for the environmental community, the council passed the new ordinance with the recommendations on January 12, 1995.

Bill Thornton, who succeeded me as mayor, pushed passage of a tree ordinance in 1996. Any new developments had to plot the trees and follow guidelines to preserve as many as possible. In May 2001 Mayor Peak led the council to pass a Unified Development

Code imposing additional regulations. With these victories under their belts, forces within the environmental community were ready to do battle over the proposed PGA Village.

But the PGA development involved more complex issues. The proposed tax district would exist for up to twenty years, whereas the forty-seven previously granted property tax abatements were for only ten years. The proposed district would also collect sales taxes and hotel-motel taxes in addition to property taxes. On the positive side, Bexar County, North East Independent School District, the Alamo Community College District, and the Bexar County Hospital District would receive their full tax allocation.

The lure of PGA of America, considered a premier sporting organization devoted to golf, explained why business leaders supported such large tax incentives. They felt the PGA courses would bring big-spending golf enthusiasts to the city. Some might even decide to move to San Antonio or relocate their businesses here.

I have never played a round of golf in my life. Not being familiar with the golf world, I was not fully convinced that PGA golf courses would provide meaningful economic impact. PGA of America had been significantly weakened in 1968 when professional tournament players broke away and formed the PGA Tour. PGA of America retained only three tournaments—the PGA Championship, the Ryder Cup, and the Senior PGA Championship. The organization owned and operated only two golf courses. But in deference to business leaders convinced that the project was important to economic development, I set aside my reservations and supported efforts to bring it to San Antonio.

The issue was extremely difficult for Garza, who was politically vulnerable. Gene Powell, his campaign finance chairman, was involved in a development next to the PGA Village and lobbied the council for support of the PGA development. To further complicate matters, Lumbermen's contracted with Garza's campaign manager, Trish DeBerry, to handle their public relations. By waiting months to play his hand, Garza turned a difficult issue into an almost impossible one. Lines had been drawn in the sand and positions hardened. The developer was not in a mode to negotiate further, and opposition groups were becoming strident.

The Smart Growth Coalition asked the council to reject the special taxing district. It sought a delay and called for a review of the land by an independent geologist. Lumbermen's opposed the independent review. Then, to put pressure on the council, Lumbermen's said that unless the district was promptly approved, it would exercise its vested property rights and build 9,000 homes on the land. It pushed council supporters to set a date for the vote. If Garza did not quickly exhibit strong leadership, he would be run over.

The Texas legislature had trumped City Hall development regulations when it granted landowners vested rights. Landowners could claim grandfathered rights if they had taken any action to develop their land before passage of a city ordinance. The action could be filing a plat, contracting for water or sewer services, or taking any number of other steps. If the landowner successfully claimed vested, or grandfathered, rights, he did not have to comply with certain new ordinances.

Many developers became more assertive in claiming their vested rights. Developer John Schaefer and his lawyer, David

Earl, filed more than a dozen lawsuits against the city claiming vested rights. Over a period of years, the city spent $1.3 million in legal fees defending itself while paying Schaefer some $3 million in court settlements.

Thus the Lumbermen's threat had teeth. They asserted they already had vested rights recognized by the city. The issue became whether a tax incentive should be used to require Lumbermen's to agree to stringent environmental restrictions. I think that if strong environmental safeguards are adopted, beyond existing regulations, then tax incentives should be considered. An example is the Westin La Cantera development, located over the Edwards recharge zone northwest of IH-10 and Loop 1604. In 1999 the council gave the 316-acre golf resort a tax abatement worth about $2.7 million over ten years. The agreement had strong environmental controls that prevented pollution of the aquifer.

On the same day as the Lumbermen's threat, Garza passed me a note during a meeting on work force development. "I want to let you know that I'll be e-mailing your office my position statement on the PGA development. Let me know your thoughts," he wrote. After reading the statement that night, I called to tell him that I supported it, and he released it the next day.

Garza demanded that the developers give 1,100 of the 2,855 acres to the city to be preserved in its natural state. He wanted hotel financing to be in place before closing, and he wanted controls over how tax money would be used. He supported the Smart Growth Coalition's demand for an independent scientific study of the property.

More than six months of debate had passed without a word

from Garza. Now he had shown leadership, but was it too late to forge a fair compromise?

The developer's six corralled votes got a little soft after Garza's statement. His strong position stymied an attempt for an early vote.

Responding to Garza's proposal, the city council commissioned a three-week study by Christopher Mathewson, a Texas A&M University engineering geologist, to evaluate the project. Although the city hired him, Lumbermen's paid him. The environmentalists were skeptical of his credentials and demanded a longer time for the review, but they lost.

On January 11, 2002, Mathewson approved the development after reviewing the studies and spending only one day on the site. Lumbermen's got the answer it wanted.

A few days later Garza showed me a memo he and five of his colleagues had signed setting a time for the council to discuss calling a sales tax election in May to buy land over the recharge zone. He thought this would appease the Smart Growth Coalition, and it in turn would support the development agreement. He was wrong. He abandoned the idea.

That night my wife, Tracy, and I attended a Western art dinner honoring Red McCombs. We sat at a table that included Jack Guenther, Kilburn Moore, and Hugo Gutierrez. Moore asked me, "Would the mayor be interested in our site for the PGA Village? Hugo and I have 3,000 acres in the vicinity of Sea World."

I set up a meeting between Moore and Garza the next day. Garza later told me the meeting went well and that he was going to Florida to see PGA officials the following week. A few days later he traveled to Port St. Lucie, the PGA headquarters. A headline the next day proclaimed that Mayor Garza said the PGA would consider a different site. I publicly backed his effort to relocate the PGA Village off the aquifer recharge zone.

Later that week my friend Cliff Morton invited me to meet Lumbermen's vice president, John Pierret, at the office of Pape-Dawson Engineers Inc. Pierret said, "We have a binding agreement with PGA for our site."

"If that's the case, why did Mayor Garza say the PGA would consider another site?" I asked.

"He wasn't listening," Pierret replied.

"It would be easier to negotiate a nonannexation agreement with the city rather than try to create an authority," I told him.

"A nonannexation agreement won't cover our cost of bringing the PGA to San Antonio," he said.

The following Tuesday the *Express-News* reported that the PGA had ruled out any other site. I had made a mistake in supporting the relocation based solely on Garza's interpretation of the PGA meeting.

In February the *Express-News* endorsed the project. Columnist Roddy Stinson followed up with a column supporting it.

Then Commissioner Tommy Adkisson came out against the project. He said the PGA was "shredding the mayor on the altar of arrogance by not considering a site off the aquifer." Archbishop Patrick Flores followed with an announcement of opposition. He said he was fearful of the threat to the city's water supply and opposed to the tax break. Reactions to his statement were mostly negative when it came to light that the Catholic Church was planning to build a new church over the recharge zone within sight of the PGA development.

Under pressure from the Smart Growth Coalition, the city council requested a legal ruling from the city attorney as to whether the development agreement would be subject to a referendum. On March 1 the city attorney ruled that it would be. With the legal opinion in hand, the coalition said it would launch a petition drive to overturn any council-approved agreement. An old saying in the real estate business is that time is the worst enemy of a real estate deal. The long delay had led to the threat of a petition drive that would kill the project.

On March 3 I went to a COPS-Metro Alliance accountability session where the groups asked all officeholders to sign a petition against the development. I was the only one to decline, and delegates booed me. But the missing mayor and council members received much harsher treatment. Ten empty baby chairs with their names attached were lined up on the stage. COPS-Metro Alliance members performed a skit with one person dressed as the "Lumbermen's King" throwing money at others who were dressed as council members. Julián Castro, the only council member to attend, received a standing ovation when he said he opposed the "Golfopolis." COPS-Metro Alliance leaders said Castro represented the whole city and not just his district.

In an attempt to structure an agreement acceptable to the Smart Growth Coalition and other concerned civic organizations, Garza and I convened a meeting with them and Lumbermen's representatives. The stakeholder organizations that attended were the Northwest Neighborhood Alliance, the Regional Clean Air and Water

Association, COPS-Metro Alliance, the Conservation Society, the Smart Growth Coalition, and the League of Women Voters. Several recommendations were made to strengthen the agreement.

A few days after the meeting Garza called me, having earlier faxed me his new twenty-two-point proposal based on feedback from stakeholder meetings. I told him I supported his proposals. At a press conference the next day he laid out his plan, which included reducing the taxing district life span to ten years, strengthening environmental standards, prohibiting the district from taking in more land, and requiring a living wage for workers.

The developers now recognized that the mayor's voice was stronger and more persuasive than any council member's. At a meeting I attended that week with the mayor and the developer's representatives, the developer quickly agreed to fourteen of the twenty-two points. Afterward we met with members of COPS-Metro Alliance, who said they would consider canceling participation in the petition drive if the council would follow the mayor's and citizens' concerns. I was encouraged.

Garza and I then met with the *Express-News* Editorial Board, where again the mayor's plan was well received. The next day's banner headline read, "Plan may be a hole in one. Developers give Garza's golf resort ideas serious consideration." We again met with the stakeholders and gave them an update on Lumbermen's concessions. They were pleased with progress but not pleased enough.

Garza and I met again with Lumbermen's, and they accepted more concessions. Garza then met with COPS-Metro Alliance and agreed to postpone the council vote one week. He also agreed to hold meetings in each council district. The delay and additional hearings turned out to be a huge mistake.

When the revised plan, which included almost all of the mayor's twenty-two proposals, was published, George Veni, a San Antonio hydrogeologist and expert on karst aquifers, said the proposal was a significant improvement. The *Express-News* endorsed the mayor's plan.

Ten simultaneous public meetings, one in each council district, took place on April 2. When the District 5 meeting grew unruly, Councilman David Garcia pulled the microphone plug on COPS leader Father Walter D'heedene. COPS led a walkout. By calling the public hearings, Garza had played into the hands of opposition members who were not serious about a compromise. Each public hearing offered an opportunity to garner negative publicity about the proposed plan.

Two days later the final hearing and debate on the PGA development got under way at 7 P.M. in a tension-filled city council chamber. COPS-Metro Alliance and the Smart Growth Coalition led the opposition. The four other stakeholder groups dropped their opposition. Archbishop Flores announced that he was now neutral on the development.

At 2:25 A.M. the council voted 9–2 in favor of the agreement, with Castro and John Sanders casting the only dissenting votes. The vote was an incredible achievement on such a controversial issue. Garza had taken a one-sided proposal and made it into an agreement that protected the public interest. The improved agreement had changed citizens' views: early polls had shown 64 percent opposed the project, but a poll after the vote showed only 44 percent opposed it.

Public opinion polls do not mean anything to a determined opposition. Later that day the Smart Growth Coalition opened its headquarters on Main Avenue. Father D'heedene announced that COPS-Metro Alliance would have 400 volunteers to collect signatures. Opponents needed 70,000 signatures to call an election.

The mayor's hard work fashioning a compromise was about to go up in flames. He had simply waited too long. Debate had been going on for more than nine months. The opposition groups wanted to fight, not compromise.

By June 25 the Smart Growth Coalition had turned in enough signatures to call an election. City clerk Norma Rodriguez verified 77,419 signatures, making this the largest petition drive ever and forcing the council to call an election.

One month later Garza called me and said, "Pierret doesn't want a public vote. Lumbermen's will withdraw from the agreement. They may ask for a nonannexation agreement."

Lumbermen's sent the city a withdrawal letter, and city council immediately repealed the ordinance. Garza announced that he would work with Lumbermen's on a fifteen-year nonannexation agreement that was not subject to a referendum. The Smart Growth Coalition felt that the city was pulling a fast one. They filed a federal lawsuit alleging that this agreement was similar to the first and thus should be subject to a public vote.

After several months of negotiations between the city and Lumbermen's on the nonannexation agreement, Garza still could not gain city council support. On October 14 I pulled up in front of Garza's community office, located in a converted warehouse at 1344 S. Flores. This was a last-ditch attempt to garner COPS-Metro Alliance's support for the nonannexation agreement. Their support was critical: several council members said they required it to vote for the agreement.

After a general discussion, Cisneros cut it short, telling COPS leader Andy Sarabia, "You give us your bottom line, and then we'll see if we can convince Lumbermen's to accept it." COPS-Metro Alliance representatives convened in an adjoining room and returned half an hour later. Sarabia said: "We want the current living wage of $8.75 to be increased by twenty-five cents a year until the hotel opens. We want the living wage to apply to all hotel employees and to nontipped full-time PGA employees. We want all full-time employees to get full benefits." Pierret sat quietly for a while, then pushed his chair away from the table and said, "Okay." And that was it.

Ten days later the city council voted 10–1 to approve the nonannexation agreement that included the COPS-Metro Alliance demands. Castro was the lone dissenting vote.

In early December Judge Fred Biery ruled that the PGA Village proposal could proceed without a public vote. He ruled that the delayed annexation agreement was significantly different from the proposed taxing authority. The city and Lumbermen's signed the contract that day.

But then nothing happened. The year 2003 slipped by without Lumbermen's building the hotel or the golf courses. Then four months into 2004 a dust-up flared at City Hall. On April 29 anti-

PGA forces appeared before the city council alleging that city staff had made changes to the contract after the council vote. They also said the parties had missed a deadline to sign the contract. Castro, quoted as saying the PGA vote "was all about a severely flawed process," persuaded five of his colleagues to sign a memo calling for an audit of the contract.

When an announcement of the memo came out, PGA President Jim L. Awtrey sent a letter withdrawing from the project. To some people it looked like the PGA was waiting for a reason to pull out, since no work had started in the seventeen months since Lumbermen's signed the contract with the city. Others laid the blame on the six councilmen. Later the city attorney said allegations by the anti-PGA forces were false and the contract was valid. The auditor said it was inappropriate to audit a contract that had not been implemented.

Tracy and I were out of town when the blowup occurred. When we returned I called Awtrey to tell him Garza and I wanted to take a delegation to their board meeting in Chicago to persuade them to change their mind. He replied, "I'm 90 percent sure the board will not reconsider. However, I have made contact with the PGA Tour. They may be interested in taking our place." I then called a press conference and announced that we would try to revive the project.

On June 8 Commissioner Lyle Larson, businessman Ernesto Ancira, former commissioner Mike Novak, DeBerry, Councilman Carroll Schubert, state Sen. Jeff Wentworth, Cisneros, and I flew to Chicago. After we each gave a pitch for San Antonio and turned over 6,000 letters of support, Awtrey said, "There are other opportunities for us, and we want to move on." But after the meeting, he whispered to me, "The PGA Tour is interested."

When we arrived home empty-handed, it was time for the media to lay blame. One doesn't get hurt politically by opposing a project that goes ahead. But when a major project is defeated there are political consequences. The *Express-News* Editorial Board laid the blame on Castro, and Stinson wrote: "Castro's memo was the straw that finally broke the project's back. The independent analysis was clearly designed to give aid, comfort and credence to San Antonio's anti–North Side screechers."

After the uproar settled down, officials of the PGA Tour Golf Course Properties quietly came to town in late June to look at the Lumbermen's site. After they toured it, Larson and I met with them at the offices of Pape-Dawson Engineers, Inc. President Vernon Kelly Jr. said:

> We like San Antonio. It's a great destination city. The site has excellent terrain for a golf course. We will start an intensive economic analysis of the project and at its conclusion will let you know if we're interested in proceeding. If we proceed we'll build two TPA [Tournament Players Association] courses, a first-class clubhouse, and a golf academy on the site. All our golf courses are built with the environment first in mind. We'll have a much larger economic impact on San Antonio than PGA of America. The PGA Tour holds over a hundred major professional golf tournaments.

After a more in-depth conversation with Kelly, I had no doubt that we were now dealing with the superior golf organization. San

Antonio has had a long history of PGA tournaments. In 1916, the year the PGA was organized, the first eighteen-hole municipal golf course in Texas was opened at Brackenridge Park, designed by golf course architect A. W. Tillinghast. In 1922 the first PGA Texas Open took place at Brackenridge and continued to be played there until 1959.

In 1922 Oak Hills Country Club opened, and it has been the site of several Texas Open tournaments. Arnold Palmer, who became the first pro to earn more than $1 million during his career, won the 1961 and 1962 Texas Open there. I have lived in a house off the Oak Hills golf course since 1989. I have watched some of the Texas Open events and found them enjoyable, though my knowledge of golf is limited. At one of the events, I met former president Gerald Ford. I have also jogged the course early in the morning for the past seventeen years. Majestic oaks, manicured greens, long fairways, birds chirping, deer grazing, squirrels squawking, an occasional coyote howl, and the delightful sighting of a fox start my day on a positive note. Two small tranquil ponds offer me the occasional opportunity to see a visiting heron. Why wouldn't a city want several of these green oases?

Today the Texas Open, which has the longest tenure of any PGA Tour event in the same city, is played at La Cantera golf courses. Former Valero Energy CEO Bill Greehey and former AT&T CEO Ed Whitacre Jr. committed their companies to become major sponsors of the Texas Open. The Senior PGA Tour, established in 1980, is at Oak Hills.

We were able to keep the PGA Tour meeting quiet for a month. Then *Express-News* reporters Greg Jefferson and Raul Dominguez wrote that the PGA Tour might come to San Antonio. While the first article was positive, we knew the negative would come, and the following day it did. The environmentalists said they would continue to oppose the development.

On September 8 Garza and I traveled to the Austin headquarters of Temple-Inland, the parent company of Lumbermen's. We wanted to see its headquarters because the site had been developed with a 15 percent impervious cover (the amount of land covered by roads, buildings, and parking lots), the standard demanded by environmentalists. We also wanted to meet with Kenny Jastrow, president of Temple-Inland, to gauge his personal commitment.

Jastrow met us on the top floor and said, "Look out the window to see what a property looks like with 85 percent of the land not built on." As we looked out the window, Garza said, "This is what we want in San Antonio. A 15 percent impervious cover would overcome the environmentalists' opposition."

"We can do that if you give us a twenty-five-year nonannexation agreement," Jastrow said.

"I think we can do that," Garza said.

About thirty days later I received a call from Arthur Coulombe, general manager for the local Marriott hotels. "Bill Marriott would like to have lunch with you and Mayor Garza here at our hotel," he said. Marriott is chairman and CEO of Marriott Hotels International, a chain of 472 hotels. Marriott has the greatest number of hotel rooms in San Antonio in its 15 hotels, including the 1,000-room Marriott Rivercenter.

On October 15 Garza and I joined Bill Marriott; his son, David; senior vice presidents Chris Rose and Charlotte Allo Collier; and

Coulombe for lunch in a private room in the hotel. The great kings of England could not have had a better meal, served in such grand fashion. Seven chefs in their toques individually served our entrées. With a smile and perhaps a little embarrassment, Bill Marriott, an unassuming man of about seventy-five, said, "I want you to know that I don't normally dine like this."

I asked him how he built such a great company. He said:

My mother and dad opened a nine-stool A&W soda fountain on Fourteenth Street in Washington in May 1927. When the weather got cold, they added chili, tamales, and tortillas. Over time they expanded to more than a hundred locations. In 1957 my dad built a 365-room hotel in Arlington, Virginia. I had just come home from the Navy and was put in charge of hotel operations. I've been building them ever since.

Halfway through the entrée, the conversation turned to the PGA development, and Marriott said, "You have a great city, and I believe it's going to get better. I like the site and would like to build a resort hotel here. Before making a decision we need to complete our financial and market analysis." Garza asked if it would be possible to complete it before the end of the year, and Marriott said he thought so. We talked about how the PGA Tour course could make San Antonio a golf destination and take us to a new level in tourism.

Garza and I had now had met with the top executives of both Temple-Inland and the Marriott. Things were falling into place. In early November we had lunch with PGA Tour officials at the Marriott Rivercenter hotel. We had assembled twenty community leaders, including Greehey, McCombs, and AT&T executive John Montford. Kelly and five other PGA Tour officials and representatives from Marriott and Lumbermen's joined us. I kicked off the meeting, and Garza spoke of his support for the project, saying he would like to conclude the agreement by the end of January.

Kelly told the group, "If we can get clarification on the environmental issues with SAWS, we could make an announcement in early January." He invited a San Antonio delegation to visit the tour's headquarters.

Express-News columnist Stinson later wrote a column predicting our chances of passing the agreement in the next few weeks as slim to none. "Read my lips," he wrote. "I-t a-i-n'-t g-o-n-n-a h-a-p-p-e-n." He added that Garza and I were drinking too much pre-holiday eggnog.

At 6 A.M. on December 3, Novak, San Antonio Greater Chamber of Commerce president Joe Krier, UT Health Science Center president Dr. Francisco Cigarroa, Hispanic Chamber president A. J. Rodriguez, and I boarded a charter flight to the PGA Tour headquarters in Ponte Vedra Beach, Florida. There we joined Garza, Councilmen Chip Haass and Richard Perez, Assistant City Manager Chris Brady, and Kelly to make our pitch to Tim Finchem, PGA Tour commissioner.

Finchem said: "There are some issues and challenges ahead. I'd like to locate in San Antonio, but first I want to see how the political process is handled." Then he excused himself. Garza told Kelly he wanted a council vote on January 6. Everything would have to fall in place for the mayor to meet his goal, but he had learned that cries for delay mean a proposal's defeat. He was not going to let grass grow under his feet this time.

Back home I convened the first of several meetings of key PGA supporters in DeBerry's office. The group included Montford, Haass, Schubert, Valero Energy Corp. executive Jim Greenwood, Rodriguez, Coulombe, and others. We approved a pamphlet that set out environmental controls to be instituted and outlined the PGA Tour's economic impact on the city. We also organized a grassroots campaign to encourage council support.

Castro, who had opposed the original PGA of America proposal, also traveled to the PGA Tour headquarters. After returning home he announced that he could support the agreement if it included a 15 percent impervious cover and the living-wage provision.

At our December 20 strategy meeting Haass said: "I believe Patti [Councilwoman Radle] will vote no. Roger [Councilman Flores] will vote for whoever gets to him last. You can count on Julián. Everyone else is a definite yes vote." DeBerry told us that Marriott, the PGA Tour, and Lumbermen's had reached an agreement in principle to build an 800-room JW Marriott Resort Hotel and two Tournament Players Association golf courses. Things were really looking good.

Later that week we met with *Express-News* Publisher Larry Walker and the *Express-News* Editorial Board, Editor Bob Rivard, columnist Stinson, and several reporters. This was the largest gathering of newspaper personnel I had seen in an editorial board meeting. After we all made our pitches, we answered questions for approximately an hour.

Why a twenty-five-year nonannexation agreement? "We need additional time to recoup our investment by agreeing to build on only 15 percent of our property," Pierret answered.

When does the nonannexation agreement start? "When we complete construction," he replied.

How does the retention/closed loop irrigation system work? "We'll lay down an impermeable clay base first," Kelly said. "Then we'll install an irrigation system that will carry the first flush off the golf course which carries the most pollutants."

How many permanent jobs? Pierret told the group that 2,000 jobs would be created, adding, "We'll pay the living wage."

What would the city give up in ad valorem taxes? "Over twenty-five years, the city would give up $44 million," Pierret said. "All other taxing entities including schools will receive $667 million during the twenty-five years."

After the meeting, as he was holding the door for the elevator, Stinson said to me, "All I've wanted was the numbers. I'm satisfied. You did a very good job, but you won't read about it in my column."

At the January 4 city council public hearing more than 80 percent of those attending supported the project. Finally, early in the morning of January 7, the council voted 10–1 for the project. Radle voted no.

Express-News columnist Ken Rodriguez wrote that we were able to secure approval of the PGA Tour project within seven months without all the acrimony and division that doomed the PGA Village. He said it could be considered masterful planning or a sneak attack. Sports columnist Richard Oliver wrote that the

PGA Tour would help San Antonio become one of the nation's foremost golf destinations, a golf capital of the Southwest.

After more than three years of political battles, it appeared we had finally crossed the finish line. But instead Marriott and Lumbermen's pushed the line back a bit. In late March I received a call from Kaufman. He said: "Marriott had agreed to pay a resort fee to Lumbermen's, to pay for the PGA golf courses. A resort fee has been ruled unconstitutional in another state. Marriott believes this will happen in Texas. We'll need to pass legislation that will allow the county to act as a pass-through agent for the resort fee." I laughed and said, "You guys are like a recurring nightmare. Bring your people over, and we'll meet."

I had been critical of the Cibolo Canyon Conservation and Improvement District bill, which had given the developers control of both taxes and projects built in the area. If we did anything, I wanted the county, not the developers, to be in control. I asked our legal team to look into the county's public improvement district law to see how we could strengthen it.

Our Bexar County team met with the Lumbermen's and Marriott teams, who told us they wanted powers similar to those under the Cibolo Canyon Conservation and Improvement District. After our team adjourned to my office, I told Ed Schweninger, chief of Bexar County's civil section, and his assistant, attorney Scott Oliver, "Draw up a bill that puts all the power in Commissioners Court. Also make it broad enough to apply to any area of the county."

When I told Kaufman of our proposal the following Monday he said, "Lumbermen's won't go for that."

"They don't have a choice," I said.

He agreed to talk with them.

Later that day Tracy and I went to Austin with our friends John and Debbie Montford to attend the Texas Medal of Arts' annual recognition of outstanding Texas artists. Debbie chaired the Texas Cultural Trust, sponsor of the affair. Our friends San Antonio singer Vicki Carr and author Naomi Shihab Nye were honored. On the trip I asked John to help me on the PGA effort. He had served fourteen years in the Texas Senate, seven of them as chairman of the Senate Finance Committee, and he knew everyone who was serving in the legislature. He agreed to help.

Montford and I met separately with Senators Madla, Wentworth, and Judith Zaffirini and Rep. Robert Puente, dean of the House delegation, to enlist their support. They said they would work with us on the legislation but warned that it would be very hard to pass this late in the session.

On April 7 Montford and I, along with the county's legal team, met with Lumbermen's and Marriott's representatives at the Greater Chamber's conference room. I said, "This will be a county effort. I don't want to see the fingerprints of Lumbermen's on this legislation." Bob Randolph, an attorney for Lumbermen's, laughed and started wiping his fingerprints off the copy before him. "We only have fifty-four days left in the session," Montford said. "This will be tough."

The following Tuesday, Commissioners Court gave approval to our legislative lobbyists to support the proposed legislation. No one from the media reported on our initiative.

Wentworth filed SB 1879 on April 21. I called Bruce Gibson,

chief of staff for Lt. Gov. David Dewhurst, and asked him to refer the bill to Madla's Intergovernmental Relations Committee as soon as possible. He did. Madla set a hearing for the bill before his committee on April 28. I spoke in favor of it. We had no opposition, and the bill passed out of his committee.

The headline in the next day's paper read, "PGA Tour tax district sought." The following day the headlines screamed, "Activists shocked by bill for PGA taxing district" and "PGA district unknown to public." Reporters accused me of covering up the effort to introduce the bill. It's true that I did not broadcast the effort, but I did mention it in court a week earlier.

On May 3 Garza, Pierret, Mitchell, and I met with the *Express-News* Editorial Board. After we explained, Walker said, "So Marriott wants assurance that the resort fee tax is legal before they will sign an agreement with Lumbermen's?"

"Yes," I said. "You're exactly right."

Walker had cut to the chase, and we came away feeling that we had made our case. Later the *Express-News* endorsed the legislation. The editorial read, "The process gives us heartburn, but the district itself does not." Columnist Lynnell Burkett wrote that I should have called a press conference to announce that we would seek the legislation. I suppose she was right.

Twelve days after the bill passed out of committee, Dewhurst set the bill for Senate consideration. The Senate passed it on May 10. We then called Speaker Tom Craddick's office to ask him to refer the bill quickly to the Natural Resources Committee, chaired by Puente. Craddick immediately referred the bill, and Puente set a hearing for May 16.

The weekend before the hearing, as I traveled to the coast, I spent the car trip talking by phone to members of our legislative delegation. When I called Puente he told me, "The more I read the bill the more I don't like it." I wondered what was going through his mind. If the House sponsor had qualms about the bill, we were in trouble. "John and I will be in Austin Monday morning to meet with you," I told him.

On Monday Montford, Mitchell, Schweninger, and I had an hourlong meeting with Puente. He outlined several changes he wanted, among them strengthening a conflict of interest provision, requiring an election in the district to impose taxes, and enlarging the board. We readily agreed to them.

While the changes were being made, I went to the House floor to meet with members of Puente's committee. As a former member of both the House and the Senate, I can go on the floor of both chambers. I talked with several representatives. Fort Worth Rep. Charlie Geren told me he did not want Tarrant County in the bill. I called Mitchell and told him to take out Tarrant County. Former Speaker Pete Laney, whom I have known since I was elected to the Senate in 1973, agreed to help.

Puente's committee would meet after the House adjourned, but the session dragged on because members were debating the issue of abortion. Finally, at 7 P.M., we received a call while we waited at the office of our lobbyist, Angelo Zottarelli. When we arrived at the committee meeting, we found our bill buried among several others pending before the committee. It came up about 9 P.M. Puente laid out the committee substitute. Montford, Milton Guess, who represented the tourism industry, and I spoke in favor of the bill. Several members of the Smart Growth Coalition spoke against it.

Our team went for a late dinner about 10:30 P.M., and while we were eating, we got a call saying the committee passed the bill.

Two days later I was back in Austin. Puente came up to me while I was visiting with some of our delegation on the House floor and said, "I'm thinking about offering a floor amendment to require a countywide vote." I replied, "I'd rather you kill the bill." He smiled and said nothing. This was the second time he'd raised issues about the bill. I thought he was teasing me. But then again he may have been serious.

I asked Rep. Joe Straus to ask his friend Rep. Beverly Woolley, chair of the Calendar Committee, to get an early setting for House action. He agreed to do so, and the bill was set for House consideration on May 22. It reached the House floor at 9:21 P.M. Fort Worth Rep. Lon Burnam raised a point of order from the back microphone, and a cluster of representatives surrounded the parliamentarian waiting for a ruling. While the ruling was pending, Wentworth came over to the House floor to talk to Burnam. He later told me how the conversation played out.

"Why are you doing this?" he said. "You don't represent Bexar County."

"Why do Palestinian children throw rocks?" Burnam said.

"What does that have to do with it?"

"Everything."

"How's that?" Wentworth said.

"Because that's all they can do. The leadership treats me the same way here, and that's all I can do—throw rocks."

Puente talked to Burnam and then announced that they had agreed to postpone the bill until the next day. They wanted to try to reach a compromise. Burnam's only compromise was to demand a countywide election. I voiced my opposition. The only people this bill would affect were those who chose to live in the proposed development. The bill did not have a countywide effect, and it would be expensive and inappropriate for a countywide vote.

Interestingly, Burnam's demand was the same one Puente had mentioned earlier that week. Did he offer the idea to Burnam? Or did Rep. Mike Villarreal, who earlier told me he was against the bill? Did San Antonio's activists get to Burnam? That's a fascinating aspect of the legislative process. You never know for sure who does you in.

Stymied in the House, I met on Monday morning with Wentworth and Sen. Jon Lindsay. Lindsay was carrying HB 2120, dealing with county government. He agreed to accept the content of our bill as an amendment to his. If Burnam's point of order was sustained, we would have a vehicle to send back to the House.

The following day, during a Commissioners Court meeting, I received a call from Puente's office telling me the House parliamentarian had sustained Burnam's point of order and SB 1879 was dead. I announced the news to the court.

The next day, a Wednesday, Montford called to say that Lindsay had accepted Wentworth's amendment containing the content of our bill. Sixteen other amendments had been added before the bill passed the Senate, expanding it from seventeen pages to more than a hundred. The bill had become what legislators call a "Christmas tree" because it contained the content of bills that had faced certain death. Each now had a gleam of life plugged in as part of a very bright tree.

After the Senate passed the bill, Houston Rep. Alma Allen, House sponsor, faced the task of trying to persuade the House to concur in all the Senate amendments. If that happened, the legislative battle was over. But if the House made changes, the bill would have to go to a conference committee. As soon as the bill came up on the House floor Friday, several supporting members clustered around the back mike to block anyone from calling a point of order.

Burnam was later quoted as saying, "I think, parliamentary maneuver-wise, I got busted. But I don't think they were playing fair and square." Rep. Patrick Rose was quoted as saying, "When you're not the first person at the microphone, you're not recognized."

Craddick called for a voice vote and, with a quick gavel, announced that the bill passed. But it had been stripped of two of the Senate's amendments, so the bill went to a conference committee. Craddick and Dewhurst quickly announced the committee members. We now ran into a major battle between Lindsay and Craddick. Craddick told his conferees he did not want the two amendments restored to the bill, but those two were the only ones Lindsay really cared about.

On Saturday I called Lindsay to thank him for supporting our measure and to say I hoped the differences could be worked out. He called back and said, "I'm sorry, but I have a major issue with the speaker." Later that day I called Wentworth, one of five senators appointed to the conference committee. He said, "I asked him

[Lindsay] to let me sponsor the bill since he no longer supported it. He refused."

Wentworth gave me Lindsay's portable number, and I left a message saying I hoped he would let Jeff pick up the bill. I told him we would give a parade in his honor in San Antonio if he would allow the bill to pass. On Sunday morning, the last day to pass the bill, I talked to Wentworth. He said, "I filed the conference report last night without Lindsay's signature. As chairman of the conference committee, Lindsay asked the clerk to give the bill back to him. Dewhurst is going to convene a Senate caucus. I'm going to seek approval to take over the bill."

In the evening Sen. Leticia Van de Putte called me. "All the senators backed Jeff, but only Lt. Gov. Dewhurst can make the final decision to recognize him to bring up the bill."

Meanwhile everything was going well in the House. About 9 P.M. Rep. Jose Menendez called. "The conference committee report was just reported to the floor," he said, "and we passed it."

I talked to Marriott's lawyer, Bebb Francis, at about 10:15. He said, "Bill Marriott had a great conversation with Lt. Gov. Dewhurst. Dewhurst called Wentworth and Lindsay in. Wentworth apologized for trying to go around Lindsay. I believe Dewhurst will recognize Wentworth if Lindsay refuses to cooperate. We have one hour and fifty minutes left in the session."

I kept looking at my watch. The minutes ticked by. At 11:30 I thought we were dead. Then I got a burst of calls at the same time, and several went to voice mail. At 11:35 Van de Putte's call came through. From the Senate floor she said, "Lindsay has just been recognized on the bill. We'll pass it in a few minutes."

At about 11:40 Wentworth called and said, "We just passed the PGA bill." Then Francis called and said, "The bill has just passed." Lomi Kriel, an *Express-News* reporter, left a voice mail asking me to call her back.

At midnight Van de Putte called and said with a laugh, "We passed the bill twenty minutes before the session ended. What was the rush? You could write a chapter on this."

Little did she know that I was writing the chapter as I was talking to her. At 12:30 A.M., exhausted and content, I shut the computer down, turned off the phone, and went to bed.

Our Bexar County legislative team led by Mitchell and Leilah Powell did a great job. Jody Richardson took the lead for Lumbermen's while Lynn Sherman, Janis Carter, Bebb Francis, and Wendy Foster worked on the Marriott team. Puente and Wentworth did the seemingly impossible by passing the legislation.

Over the next several months Marriott, the PGA, and Lumbermen's had to renegotiate their contract under the terms of the new public improvement district. Commissioners Court had to create the special district and name a seven-member board to administer it.

At a September public hearing, only one person spoke in opposition to the district. Either we had worn out its opponents or they had concluded that the project was environmentally sound. After the hearing we passed an order granting petition for the creation of the Cibolo Canyon Special Improvement District; appointment of directors and imposition of ad valorem, sales and use, and hotel occupancy taxes; and authority to enter into economic development agreements, grants, and loans. We appointed a board that included automobile dealer Ernesto Ancira, former city council-woman Lynda Billa Burke, attorney Walter Serna, Valero executive Keith Booke, investment banker Robert Rodriguez, International Bank of Commerce executive Jon Nixon, and SBC executive Jim Callaway. We later passed an order calling an election to confirm the district and its taxing and economic development authority.

When the board met on September 6, I told them: "Your duties are similar to a city council in terms of the power to tax and spend. No other district in Texas has the power you do. It's your responsibility to use your authority to protect the public interest."

The board chose Ancira as president and Burke as vice president. It set November 8 for a special election within the district to authorize creating the public improvement district. It also began working with the developer on a comprehensive economic development agreement.

The board developed a plan providing that property taxes would pay for streets, drainage, sewer, and water lines. The hotel-motel tax and the sales tax would be used for economic development, with most of it paying for the two golf courses. The plan included setting aside 700 acres of land for preservation and allowing only 15 percent impervious cover.

An *Express-News* story reported that only five people who lived in trailers on site would be eligible to vote. I knew this would sound bad, but it has happened more than 1,200 times in special district elections in other communities. All five residents voted early, making for an anticlimactic election day. The initiative, nevertheless, passed with a unanimous vote.

Over the next two months we began intensive negotiations

over the final agreements to implement the plan developed earlier by the board of the public improvement district. Mitchell and Oliver became the principal negotiators on our behalf. On January 9, 2006, the board ratified the agreements, followed by Commissioners Court three days later. We added a more aggressive minority contracting provision.

Surely this would be the end of the process. But it was not to be. New problems arose as Marriott began negotiating the final details of its agreement with Lumbermen's. Negotiations dragged on for months. During this time, Marriott reached an agreement with a hotel developer to build and own the hotel, which Marriott would operate. The developer's lender demanded a change in the city's nonannexation agreement. Although the change was minor, having to go back to the city council presented a huge problem.

Mayor Phil Hardberger was not delighted to be handed a worn-out hot potato. He had opposed the PGA project during his mayoral campaign. In our weekly meeting, when I pushed him on the issue, he said, "It would be difficult to change even non-controversial parts of the agreement." When the problem became public, *Express-News* columnist Carlos Guerra wrote, "Close to Halloween, the PGA monster rears it ugly head."

In October I sat next to City Manager Sheryl Sculley at a civic luncheon and asked her how the talks with Marriott were going. She said, "I talked to Chris Rose." Rose was in charge of the Marriott project. "He told me the hotel will be a step above the Desert Ridge Resort and Spa in Phoenix. I worked with him on that project. I trust him. We'll get the changes worked out."

My son Kevin, a city councilman representing the area where

the PGA Village will be built, went to work securing council votes. He negotiated an agreement with Lumbermen's that called for a stronger living-wage provision and for 130 additional acres of parkland. Marriott, in turn, received an extra six months to start construction and an extra eighteen months to complete construction. The agreement included a provision that the golf courses could use Edwards Aquifer water instead of Trinity well water. It did not change the length of the nonannexation pact.

The council, after five hours of debate, passed the changes 8–3 on October 12. After the vote, Rose called and said, "We're going to have a groundbreaking early next year. This project is now a go."

But the groundbreaking was a long time coming, as had been every other step with the PGA Village. More than six months later Pierret told me: "I'm leaving for Washington this Sunday. All the principals from Marriott, their lender, their developer, and my company will meet Monday to sign the final documents. We plan to have a groundbreaking on the first Friday in May."

Another problem forced yet another delay. The legislative bill that set out the bonding capacity was ambiguous. The 2007 Texas legislature would have to correct it. But it was just a technical correction—no reason to worry. I received a called from Francis on May 15, just two weeks before the legislature was scheduled to adjourn. "Robert says he doesn't support the correction," he said. "Will you call him?" Puente laughed when I called him, and I could tell he was twisting their tail. He supported the change as a floor amendment to HB 3223, and it passed.

Then I received another call from Francis. He said he had

received six boxes containing all 465 documents that had finally been signed by Marriott, Miller Global (the builder and owner of the hotel), Forestar (Lumbermen's had changed its name), and the PGA Tour. He had to pay County Clerk Jerry Rickoff $11,000 in filing fees for sixty-four of the documents.

By fall 2007 I had been involved as county judge in the PGA battle for over six years, the longest sustained controversial struggle I've ever been part of. On several occasions I had my doubts that the project would be built. But the longer the struggle went and the more difficult it was, the more determined I became. There is something to be said for tenacity.

This story came to a happy ending on October 18, 2007, on a bright sunny day on a hilltop in the PGA village. As I got out of my car and walked across the site where the 1,002-room Marriott resort hotel would be built and looked around at the beautiful site where the two TPC golf courses were being constructed, I was glowing inside.

Gathered under a tent were hundreds of people celebrating the long-awaited groundbreaking. All the major principals were there. I greeted PGA Tour Commissioner Tim Finchem, Marriott International CEO Bill Marriott, Temple-Inland CEO Kenny Jastrow, and Miller Global CEO Jim Miller. Mingling among the crowd were some of the key players—Bill Kaufman, Seth Mitchell, John Pierret, Chris Rose, Trish DeBerry, and Sen. Jeff Wentworth. Golf legend Pete Dye attended; he and Greg Norman will design the two courses. PGA golfer Bruce Lietzke, who along with Sergio Garcia will be player consultants for the courses, was there.

After we gave our speeches, we lined up and simultaneously hit a sand wedge for a nice photo op. And that was it.

Although our groundbreaking was symbolic, work was already progressing on the golf courses and the hotel. They'll both open in March 2010. See you there.

THREE
· · · · · · · · · · ·
Toyota

WHO WOULD HAVE BELIEVED that in less than five short
months a city could alter its future and a major international corporation could adjust its course for the coming century?

That is the story of San Antonio's courtship of Toyota Motor
Corp., which took place from August 2002 to February 2003.
What happened behind the scenes during those frantic, exhilarating months led to a marriage of interests that continues to play out
to the benefit of all concerned.

During the first week of August 2002, Mario Hernandez, president of the San Antonio Economic Development Foundation
(EDF), called me. Toyota Motor Corp. was considering a North
Side site near the city of Schertz as a possible location to manufacture its Tundra pickup. "Toyota doesn't want publicity," he said.
"We've named the project Star Bright. If Toyota considers the site
feasible, they'll want to meet with you."

Hernandez was used to privacy requests. Since 1975, when
Gen. Robert McDermott, then chairman of USAA, had founded
the EDF, it had worked to recruit companies that would consider
moving to San Antonio or relocating a facility here. Proposed

relocations are highly sensitive to the companies, and secrecy is a must.

The news was stunning. An automobile manufacturing plant in San Antonio? That hardly seemed likely. Texas attracted its last auto plant some forty years ago when General Motors located one in Dallas. Over the years San Antonio had made several unsuccessful attempts to lure one. In 1986 we tried to get a Saturn plant, and in 1993 we made an unsolicited bid for Mercedes-Benz. We had tried for a Hyundai manufacturing plant earlier in 2002. Most companies located their plants in the Midwest, close to their supply lines and good rail infrastructure.

In fact, most of our efforts to attract any type of manufacturing had resulted in failure. Following the U.S. trend that showed a loss of more than 2.8 million manufacturing jobs from 2000 to 2003, local manufacturing jobs had dropped from 7.4 percent to 6.1 percent in the same time span. In 1995, when the government decided to close Kelly Air Force Base, a logistics base that performed significant airplane repair and modification work, we knew we could no longer rely on the military for manufacturing. The city took over operation of Kelly, turning it into an industrial park. Several firms, including the Boeing Company and Lockheed Corp., located there. But these companies merely replaced some of the manufacturing work that Kelly employees had done for years.

If we could attract the crown jewel of manufacturing, an automobile manufacturing plant, we would dramatically change our local economy. According to then Texas Comptroller Carole Rylander, such a plant would lead to the creation of 12,000 jobs, a nearly $1 billion increase in personal income, and more than $1.5

billion in related investment. Some ten to twenty parts manufacturing companies could follow a plant. Furthermore, not just any motor company was looking at us. Toyota was the champion of them all, a company with a market value that exceeded the combined total of General Motors, Ford, and Chrysler. Toyota was the undisputed leader of the worldwide automobile industry.

After hearing from Hernandez, I read everything I could get my hands on about Toyota. What a fascinating story I uncovered. The company traces its beginning to Sakichi Toyoda, who was born in 1867 in the small farming village of Yamaguchi, Japan. He was trained as a carpenter, but at the age of eighteen he decided he wanted to be an inventor. He built a successful model for a wooden cloth-making loom and eventually founded the Toyoda Automatic Loom Works, patenting many of his processes. He established his business on the principle of Kaizen, which means incremental, continuous improvement. He believed there were always better ways to manufacture, and he was determined to find them. This principle would become the guiding light for Toyota.

When he died in 1930, Toyoda left one million yen to his son Kiichiro, a trained engineer. He made clear that the money could be used only to start an auto manufacturing business. In a small corner of the loom manufacturing plant, Kiichiro began his research, producing the first prototype car in 1935 and truck in 1936. In 1937 he and Risaburo Toyoda, his brother-in-law, took Toyota Motor Company, Ltd. public. He used the name Toyota, which has eight Japanese brushstrokes, instead of the family name Toyoda, which has ten brushstrokes. Eight was a lucky number in Japan, one that signified growth. He grabbed hold of lady luck.

Toyota's first plant opened on rural land near Koromo, Japan. After Risaburo died, Kiichiro and his cousin Eiji ran the business. Kiichiro died in 1952, and his twenty-seven-year-old son Shoichiro joined the firm that year. In 1957 the company built Toyota City near Nagoya in southern Japan. Parts manufacturers and suppliers located around the manufacturing plant, and Toyota took part ownership of many of its suppliers. In 1955 Toyota exported its first car, the Crown, to the United States, and in 1957 the company founded Toyota Motor Sales, USA.

Throughout the 1950s the Big Three American motor companies dominated the industry. They were so powerful that they ignored the advice of W. Edwards Deming, who advocated quality-controlled production. While the Big Three ignored Deming, the Japanese automobile industry took his advice. Toyota did it best. In 1965 the company won the coveted W. Edwards Deming prize for quality control.

In 1982 Shoichiro Toyoda became president of the company. Under his leadership, Toyota opened its first manufacturing plant in North America in 1984 in a joint venture with General Motors. One of the Americans involved in that initial venture was a thirty-five-year-old lawyer named Dennis Cuneo, who later would become important to San Antonio's quest for a Toyota plant. Cuneo had first met Toyota officials while he was an attorney in the Washington, D.C., law firm of Arent, Fox, Kintner, Plotkin and Kahn. By 2002 Toyota had invested $13.8 billion in manufacturing plants in North America, employing 34,000 people and producing 1.2 million vehicles annually. The company had plants in California, Indiana, Kentucky, and Ontario, Canada. The United

States had become Toyota's largest market, and it was projected to continue growing. Demographers predicted that the U.S. population would increase to more than 400 million people by 2030, while Japan would begin losing population in 2007. Thus, from both political and logistical standpoints, building cars in the company's most important emerging market made sense.

During the last two decades, San Antonio officials had worked hard to foster strong commercial and friendship ties with Japan. The relationship began when Mayor Henry Cisneros led a trade delegation to Japan in 1985. As a result of that trip, San Antonio developed a sister-city relationship with Kumamoto in 1987, and while I was a member of the city council we approved the relationship. Sister-city relationships are important because they open the door to understanding each other's culture, resulting in friendships and building trust. If all goes well, trade may follow.

In the mid-1980s Cisneros met Seiichi and Naoko Shirane and hired them to represent San Antonio in Japan. Mrs. Shirane was well connected to industry and political leaders there. A member of the Mitsui family, which had once controlled major banking and industrial companies, she was also a first cousin to Hiroko Toyoda, wife of Shoichiro. Her husband, Seiichi, was connected to royalty. His great-grandfather was a baron and one of the first ministers of the Meiji Cabinet. The Shiranes met when they both worked for Gen. Douglas MacArthur in his postwar administration in Japan. After her husband's death in 1990, Mrs. Shirane continued to work for the city.

Since Cisneros opened the door to Japan, all subsequent mayors have worked to solidify the relationship. Mayors Lila Cockrell,

Bill Thornton, Howard Peak, Ed Garza, Phil Hardberger, and I have led trade delegations to visit there. When, as mayor, I traveled to Japan with Mrs. Shirane in 1992, I met with several Japanese business leaders, including Akio Morita, the founder and CEO of Sony. I also traveled to our sister city, Kumamoto. As a result of all these efforts, several Japanese firms have located in San Antonio. Sony Semiconductor, Colin Medical Instruments, and Takata Seatbelts have built plants here, although the Sony plant is no longer in operation.

As we enhanced our relationship with Japan, we also strengthened our economic ties with Mexico. While I was mayor in the early 1990s, we became the first U.S. city to open trade offices in that country. In turn, several Mexican states opened offices in San Antonio. Our relationship with Mexico was important for Toyota because each year the company purchased about $600 million in parts from twenty different Mexican companies. They owned controlling interest in two major suppliers based in Monterrey. The Mexican states of Nuevo León and Coahuila, which border Texas, have become the largest auto-manufacturing center in Mexico.

The availability of a good work force always ranks at the top of business considerations. San Antonio has a growing work force, one that is becoming better educated. The last decade has brought a 19 percent increase in higher education attainment. By 2000 almost a quarter of the adult population had some college education, and 13.8 percent had bachelor's degrees.

Thus, if Toyota wanted to locate in Texas, it had good reasons to move to San Antonio. Its proximity to Mexico, its growing young educated work force, and its close ties to Japan were all assets. Plus, Texas is the nation's largest purchaser of pickups, accounting for more than 20 percent of total U.S. pickup sales.

The state had negatives as well. Economist M. Ray Perryman's research found Texas lagging far behind in competing for manufacturers because its tax structure places disproportionate burdens on capital-intensive industries. He recommended that Texas expand tax credits for manufacturing and implement a deal-closing fund.

Texas faced tough competition for a plant. Toyota was also considering sites in Arkansas, Mississippi, and Tennessee. Those sites all had excellent rail and highway systems. They were located in the heart of the nation, while Texas was on the outer edge. Those states also provided large financial incentive packages.

The day after Hernandez's initial call, he called again. "Toyota officials like the farm and ranchland south of the city," he said. "They like the flat land and the fact that there is very little development. We're going to show them some sites." While Toyota continued to look at possible sites, we began work on a proposal. I signed a thirty-five-page proposal for Toyota on August 13 that included offers of tax abatements from the city, county, and school districts, as well as a package of economic incentives from the state. The total package provided more than $100 million in economic incentives.

The next day Hernandez and I met with Mayor Garza at his office. As Hernandez showed him the proposed South Side sites on a map, I saw a frown on Garza's face. After Hernandez's presentation, Garza said, "I want to first make sure the site fits in with my South Side plan." During his mayoral campaign he had said he would work to balance growth by promoting economic development on the South Side. He wanted the growth to be planned rather than haphazard, as had occurred on the North Side.

I was concerned about Garza's comment, but had I known what he was really thinking I would have been alarmed. Later I found out that the day before we met, he wrote in his diary: "My top policy initiative had an unknown variable fall from the sky. . . . I'm picturing dirty industrial buildings, tall smokestacks and thick black fumes—possibly in the middle of my South Side Initiative." He wrote that he was not only skeptical but also angry about the Toyota proposal.

Garza's plan for the South Side was impractical without a major economic initiative, and thus I thought he would be excited about Toyota locating there. I quickly gathered my thoughts. When he finished, I said, "Ed, the Toyota plant would be a magic bullet for your plan. It's one of the most environmentally sensitive companies in the world. You need industrial development on the South Side to create good-paying jobs. People will never live there unless they have that."

Fortunately, Emil Moncivais, the city's planning director, explained that some industrial zoning would be necessary for his plan, and that the plant could be located in an area that could be buffered. He pointed out the area between Medina River and Leon Creek. After about an hour's discussion, Garza began warming to the idea. I breathed a sigh of relief. Had he not changed his mind, Toyota might never have located in San Antonio.

A week later I had lunch with Hernandez, Commissioner

Robert Tejeda, and two school superintendents from the area, Mard Herrick of Southside Independent School District and Pete Anthony of Southwest Independent School District. Both superintendents agreed to sign a letter committing to ask their respective boards to agree to abate Toyota school taxes for up to ten years. State law provided that school districts could give tax abatements without losing additional state funding.

That night Tracy and I had dinner with Red and Charlene McCombs, Tom and Nancy Loeffler, and Pat Somerall and his wife. McCombs, billionaire and at that time owner of the Minnesota Vikings football team, is a large financial supporter of Gov. Rick Perry. Loeffler is a former congressman and a close friend of President George W. Bush and Perry. Somerall is a former New York Giants football player and football announcer.

I said to McCombs and Loeffler, "Mario told me that Dennis Cuneo, the person in charge of site location, has received calls from the governors of Alabama and Kentucky but not Texas. Would one of you call Governor Perry and ask him to call Cuneo?" Loeffler said he would. The next day Mike McKinney, Perry's chief of staff, called. "Tom called me about Toyota," he said. "Governor Perry will call Dennis Cuneo." Now we were on the playing field.

Cuneo, one of the first Americans to join Toyota as part of the management team that created the 1984 joint venture with General Motors, had become senior vice president of Toyota Motor Manufacturing North America. He would determine whether San Antonio joined Team Toyota.

A few days later the governor and I talked as we flew on an SBC plane to Mexico City to pursue the Pan American Games.

"I'm going to have the Toyota incentive legislation introduced early in the next session," he told me. "I'll push for early passage." The legislature would convene for its biennial session in January, months later. Toyota would have to believe that Perry had the political muscle to pass the incentive package.

"It's my understanding that Toyota needs approval of their emission permit within five months of the application," I said. "Would you call the chairman of the Natural Resource Conservation Commission?" Perry agreed to call.

On August 30, in a conference room at San Antonio's International Center, I had my first face-to-face meeting with Toyota officials. The Toyota group included Sig Huber, assistant general counsel; Isao Tanaka, corporate affairs director; and Toshiaki Tsuji, strategic planning director. Garza and Hernandez, as well as City Manager Terry Brechtel and Jeff Moseley, director of the Texas Department of Economic Development, also attended.

Huber, who reported to Cuneo, led off by saying, "Your city is well thought of in Japan because of your long friendship." He continued, "We'll judge over the next few months whether your community really wants us. Any negative publicity will not be well received." He added that they were considering other states, as well as a site in Dallas. "We're on a fast track and would like to make a decision in December. We ask you to keep our meeting confidential."

Garza assured him of confidentiality and community support. "The city will provide at least a thousand acres of land to Toyota," he said. Huber responded that the land was a critical component of the financial package and said Toyota appreciated the generous offer. Garza had evolved from a doubter into a very aggressive suitor. His offer was extremely important because other communities had agreed to provide free sites.

In early September Toyota President Fujio Cho announced that the company might consider another manufacturing plant in the United States. A few days later, Toyota Chairman Hiroshi Okuda was quoted as saying a growing demand for cars meant that a new plant was necessary. These were the first public acknowledgments that Toyota was serious about a new plant. Four days later Governor Perry quietly met with Cuneo in Austin and assured him that Texas would put together a significant financial package.

If we were going to land Toyota, San Antonio had to overcome serious clean air problems. The Environmental Protection Agency had declared Bexar County out of compliance with the Clean Air Act. The agency's next step would be to declare the area as having nonattainment status, a designation all other large American cities had already reached and one reason Toyota located its plants in rural areas. If Bexar County reached nonattainment status, it would have trouble attracting not only Toyota but also any industry that emitted volatile organic compounds and nitric oxide. Toyota's plant would increase our local emission by 1.6 percent.

We had already been working on that problem. I and other public officials had participated in negotiating the nation's first clean air pact with the Environmental Protection Agency. On July 18, the month before the first Toyota contact, I had met with Gregg Cooke, the EPA regional director, and Bob Huston, chairman of the Texas Natural Resource Conservation Commission (which that September became the Texas Commission on Environmental Quality), and committed to enacting a local pact. We negotiated an agreement requiring us to take action to clean our air and giving us until 2007 to meet the clean air standards. In early September Commissioners Court ratified the pact. Eventually Bexar, Comal, Wilson, and Guadalupe counties and the major cities within them approved the pact. This removed a major hurdle to attracting Toyota.

The first public leak of project Star Bright appeared in the *San Antonio Express-News* on September 11. The story reported that Toyota was looking at two local sites. Garza was quoted as saying Toyota officials had met with the city's economic development staff. That same day Mike McKinney told me: "Dennis Cuneo told the governor that Toyota wanted environmental indemnification on the land. It also wants a lower electric rate and dual railroad line access." I committed to following up with both City Public Service and Garza.

The next day another Toyota team came to town, this time led by Toyota's environmental general manager, Kotaro Nakamura. He chartered a helicopter and followed the railroad tracks south. After looking at twelve potential South Side sites, he convinced Cuneo that the best location was a 2,700-acre tract facing Applewhite Road, between the Medina River and Leon Creek. Within that tract was a 1,700-acre ranch owned by the Walsh family. The ranch's roots could be traced back to Juan Ignacio Perez, a Canary Island descendant who founded the ranch in 1794. John H. Small and his wife, Patricia Walsh Small, along with his son, John E. Small, and his sister, Elizabeth, held controlling interest in the ranch. Convinced of Toyota's excellent environmental record, the

Smalls agreed to sell the land. Other family members reluctantly agreed but then later caused significant trouble. That story comes later.

The site was exclusively within the 115-square-mile boundaries of Southwest Independent School District. Of its 9,600-student population, 83.9 percent were Hispanic, and 76 percent were economically disadvantaged. The Toyota plant's impact would be huge, more than doubling the district's total property value.

That evening, at a fund-raiser for Sen. Frank Madla, I asked CPS General Manager Milton Lee about electrical rates. "We brought the electrical rate down from 3.8 cents to 3.4 cents," he said. "Try to do better," I replied. He laughed and said, "Get the city to give up its 14 percent profit."

On September 14 the *Express-News* headlined a story quoting Perry, who said Toyota would make a decision within sixty days. He said San Antonio remained the only Texas site under consideration. Toyota spokesman Dan Sieger was quoted as saying, "It would be bad business practice to discuss them [the sites]."

The governor made a mistake commenting on Toyota. The political pressure on Toyota intensified in other states it was considering. But with no other Texas site under consideration, the state could rally behind San Antonio. Garza and I pulled together a team of some sixty county, city, state, and private-sector leaders to create what became known as Team Toyota, meeting first on September 18.

Two days later Garza, EDF chairman Joe McKinney, San Antonio Greater Chamber of Commerce President Joe Krier, and I traveled together to Ray's Steak House in Austin. Greeted by owners Ray and Little Ray and led to a private dinning room, we saw Cuneo, the man who held San Antonio's fate in his hands. He was talking with Texas Economic Development director Moseley.

While we visited with Cuneo during the hour before dinner, each of us tried to make a meaningful connection with him. As we sat down to dine on huge steaks, double-thick onion rings, specialty breads, and desserts as large as the steaks, our host, Texas Association of Business President Bill Hammond, and his wife joined us. Then Garza offered a toast to Toyota, Texas, and San Antonio. Our connections were working. Cuneo seemed comfortable as he smiled and joined in the toast.

After dinner Garza asked, "How does it look for San Antonio?"

"I believe San Antonio is the right size Texas city," Cuneo said. "We like your open land south of the city. We like your culture and your work force. But there's a difference of opinion within Toyota. Our manufacturing people like the three sites in Arkansas, Mississippi, and Tennessee—good central location and close to our suppliers. Our marketing people like Texas because the people in Texas buy more pickups than in any other state. They also like the Hispanic connection. It's a growing market for Toyota. San Antonio offers us the opportunity to hire Hispanics in executive positions with the company."

When Garza asked about the key unresolved issues, Cuneo responded: "You need to get us a lower electrical rate to meet what we're paying at our Kentucky site and dual track usage of the Union Pacific tracks. Keep your clean air designation and get an option on the site that we like. Two of our board members will be in San Antonio on October 12. I can't sell them on the site unless you have an option."

Garza wanted to know if we should go to a Japan-southern U.S. conference in Houston where the president of Toyota North America, Toshiaki Taguchi, would speak.

"You can go, but it's not important," Cuneo said.

"We're planning a trip to our sister city Kumamoto," Garza said. "Should we attempt to see Toyota officials?"

"No," Cuneo said. "They wouldn't like that."

After dinner we drove Cuneo to the historic Driskill Hotel where he was staying. After we dropped him off, I said to Garza, "He's the man. He made it clear that he's in charge and that he'll drive the negotiations."

In some instances the EDF contracts with real estate brokers to deal with land purchases in order to keep the real purchaser's identity secret. Kit Corbin of Grubb and Ellis Commercial Real Estate Services put some 2,000 acres under contract with two families and the Cook Memorial Trusts. On September 24 Corbin signed three contracts under his own name. In addition to the 2,000 acres, the San Antonio Water System gave 600 acres of land directly to Toyota.

I met with Huber again, this time in my office. We went over details of the county's tax abatement policy. I told him the county would fund the $26 million in costs to improve Applewhite Road, Zarzamora Street, and Watson Road. He said he was pleased with the county package and that things looked good.

At noon on October 14, I walked into the La Babia Room

of the Westin Riverwalk hotel. Standing around the room were business leaders Bartell Zachry, Peter Holt, Tom Frost, Bob Davis, Joe McKinney, Cisneros, and McCombs. Joining them were City Manager Brechtel and EDF president Hernandez. Shortly after I arrived, Cuneo walked in with Jim Wiseman, vice president of external affairs for Toyota. As they were being introduced, Garza walked in escorted by his security people.

After we sat down Cuneo said, "The possibility of locating in Texas was an afterthought." McCombs smiled and said, "Texas, an afterthought?" Cuneo laughed and said, "Our marketing department first raised the idea of locating in Texas. We always sell more cars and trucks where we make them."

Cisneros said, "The automobile industry is peaking at about 13.9 million vehicles a year. The experts don't see much room for growth except within the Hispanic community. It's expected that Hispanics will buy an additional hundred thousand cars each year." Each one of the business leaders gave their pitch for San Antonio, and Cuneo seemed pleased.

Ten days later Garza announced to the media that he would meet with Toyota officials in Japan. When Cuneo heard about the announcement he called and told Garza to cancel the trip. Garza later put out a release saying he had canceled because of too much publicity. It was embarrassing, but it was also a good lesson in corporate politics. He never should have pursued the meeting after Cuneo said not to. Cuneo reported directly to the board in Japan. He'd asserted his power and let it be known he did not want anybody going around him.

Arkansas Gov. Mike Huckabee made the same mistake,

announcing that he would visit Toyota in Japan. An executive in Cuneo's office was quoted in the *Express-News* as saying: "We advised him against it, but he kept pushing. So we arranged for him to make a visit to Japan. I'm not sure yet who he'll be able to meet with." The governor had gotten under Cuneo's skin.

While we were working on the biggest economic development project in San Antonio's history, a bolt of lightning struck City Hall that could have killed our efforts. On October 9, as I sat down next to Commissioner Paul Elizondo during a Commissioners Court meeting, he passed me a note saying the FBI had arrested councilmen John Sanders and Enrique "Kike" Martin on bribery charges.

Then Commissioner Lyle Larson leaned over and said, "Watch this." He pulled up on his computer screen an image of Sanders walking out of City Hall in handcuffs. The FBI had made Sanders take a "perp walk." Parading him in handcuffs before the media was a dramatic way to embarrass him and call attention to what quickly would become a high-profile political and governmental scandal. This was the first time in modern history that a sitting San Antonio council member had been indicted for a felony.

Sanders was an African American pastor, well respected in his community, with a long history as an activist for social causes. I had worked with him on several city-county issues when we were building the A&T Center on the East Side. I felt sick to my stomach as I stared in disbelief at Sanders being led away.

The federal indictment charged Martin with accepting bribes totaling $7,500 and conspiracy to commit fraud. Sanders was charged with conspiring to commit bribery and two counts of accepting bribes totaling $4,500. Lawyers Juan Peña and Jack

Pytel, who represented the firm attempting to do business with the city, were charged with conspiring to commit bribery.

The next day FBI Special Agent in Charge Steve McCraw was quoted in the *Express-News* as saying, "We view it as the beginning stages of a far-reaching investigation into public corruption." He said other officials were under investigation. I immediately called Cuneo to assure him this was an isolated incident. He told me Garza had called to say he was not involved and that he thought no one else on the city council was implicated. Cuneo said to me, "I'll be looking to you to take the lead."

Less than three weeks later District Attorney Susan Reed announced a state indictment of former councilman Raul Prado, a candidate for state representative, and Martin on charges unrelated to the federal indictments. She also indicted several people in connection with a bribery scheme at the Alamo Community College District.

With the scandal surrounding him, Garza stayed focused on attracting Toyota, and we continued to work together on the project. I had talked with Huber, Toyota's lawyer, and he said we needed to solve two big problems. Union Pacific had not agreed to allow Burlington Northern Santa Fe access to its tracks. He also wanted assurances that, if the company expanded its plant, its emission permit would not be challenged. I followed up with a call to Huston, chairman of the Texas Commission on Environmental Quality. He said he would try to get a flexible permit that would allow the plant to expand. The commission eventually granted the permit.

Hernandez called to say the Toyota board's decision would be delayed until after the first of the year. "It looks like Arkansas

Governor Huckabee's pressure is paying off," I said. That afternoon Garza and I talked with Cuneo by speakerphone in the mayor's office. "The delay was caused by a leak to the media in Japan," he said, "and by politicians from other states who are weighing in. The board's final decision will be made in February."

"Can the decision be made in January?" I asked. "The legislature goes into session the second week of January and will adjourn in May. The later the decision, the harder it will be to get legislation passed."

Cuneo promised to try and then said the railroad issue still had to be resolved.

"Next week the Commissioners Court will take up the issue of creating a rail district," I told him. "If Union Pacific will not allow access to Burlington Northern, we'll build our own line."

"Good," Cuneo said. "By the way, I'm on the last chapter of your book *Mayor*. I've enjoyed it. You said something nice about Hillary Clinton. Now her husband is trying to get Toyota to locate in Arkansas. How do you like that?"

"I don't," I said, and laughed.

He said he would be in San Antonio on Monday to meet with our congressional delegation. His parting words were to keep cool.

On Sunday Garza, Cisneros, Hernandez, Loeffler, and Tracy and I met with Joe and Cyndi Krier at their home to develop a political strategy to deal with the delayed decision. Cisneros said, "If our competition is going to Japan, Governor Perry, Ed, and Nelson should also go."

"Cuneo doesn't want us to go," Hernandez said.

"He may be losing control," Cisneros said.

"I don't think so," I said. "I believe it would be a mistake to go around him. There are still some unresolved issues we need to deal with, such as dual rail access."

"I'm not sure Toyota understands the political problems of the short legislative session," Cyndi said.

Riding home after the meeting, I said to Tracy, "We've bet our whole stack on Dennis. It's too late to drop out of this pot. Every time the mayor has gone around him, it's caused trouble. I'm sticking with him."

Cuneo had to control the selection process for a very good reason. If people go around the lead person, confusion begins to permeate the organization and the lead person loses control. I experienced that when we tried to bring a Washington Mutual regional center to San Antonio. Some realtors proposed that the company buy an existing building rather than build at the planned site. This caused the company to second guess the decision to build and then to begin looking at other cities.

Garza and I met with Cuneo the following week at the Greater Chamber offices. I handed Cuneo a copy of *USA Today* with a story that San Antonio was Toyota's likely choice. He looked at it, smiled, and said, "I've seen it." He added, "I had a good meeting with your congressional delegation earlier today. They're very supportive. I think you should work on the idea of creating a supplier park on the Toyota site. This will be the largest tract of land Toyota will own anywhere in the world. They surrounded themselves with suppliers in Toyota City, but they haven't done this in the United States."

"We could create an incentive package that treats all the suppliers as one company if they co-locate," I said. "Add up the jobs and the total investment and set our incentive based on the total. We've never done that before."

"If you do that I'll try to persuade Toyota to create the park," Cuneo said. "The Toyota board will meet in the middle of January to make its decision. We'll make a public announcement on February 9 or 10."

After the meeting I knew we had made the right decision in sticking with him.

Commissioners Court instructed staff to prepare an order to create a rail district on November 13. We thought we could use it as a pressure point to get Union Pacific to allow Burlington Northern Santa Fe access on their track. Why was dual access so important? A study by *Railway Age* magazine showed that companies without dual access paid 30 to 60 percent higher freight rates. They also found that service was poorer.

Six days later I arrived at Ray's Steak House in Austin, where I had first met Cuneo. This time I was meeting with Jeff Moseley, director of the Texas Department of Economic Development, and Charles Eisele, a senior vice president for Union Pacific. After we settled in for the meal, Eisele said, "We'll guarantee Toyota competitive rates and reliable service, but we will not grant Burlington Northern access over our line."

Moseley responded, "If Toyota doesn't come to Texas, you'll be blamed."

After the meeting I called Cuneo to tell him the news. "You have to get the rail district going," he said. I told him we'd start tomorrow.

The next morning a front page story in the *Express-News* quoted Mark Davis, a Union Pacific regional spokesman, as saying, "We built it [the rail line]. Why should we let 'em [Burlington] use it?" That same day Commissioners Court created the rail district. After the vote I said, "If this project fails . . . and the only reason they [Toyota] don't come is because of Union Pacific, I think that would be a tremendous headache for that company."

In order to turn the headache up a notch, I talked to Congressmen Lamar Smith, Charlie Gonzalez, Ciro Rodriguez, and Henry Bonilla. Each committed to helping us get funds for the proposed railroad line and put pressure on Union Pacific.

The next day Cuneo told me: "Your mayor visited with Toyota officials while he was in Washington. He mentioned that Toyota would announce its decision in February. I got a call from them asking what's up. He's about to cause another delay in the decision. He needs to quit talking to other Toyota officials." Cuneo later sent a letter to Garza that read, "I am the designated lead on this project, and it causes confusion within our organization when San Antonio officials try to make contact with other Toyota officials."

On the following Monday I had lunch with Union Pacific's Eisele at the Plaza Club. He said they were working with Toyota to try to make them happy, but his company still would not allow dual rail access. After the meeting Cuneo told me he was asking Governor Perry to transfer $15 million to the rail district from the funds he'd pledged to Toyota.

"That should get Union Pacific's attention," I said.

On December 9 Ric Williamson, a Texas Department of

Transportation commissioner, told me: "I believe we've found $17 million for your rail district. We hope to make an announcement soon." "I hope it's real soon," I said. "Our rail district board will be up and operating this week." He said he might have something by week's end.

The next day, Commissioners Court appointed Bruce Flohr, Connie English, LeRoy Greene, Cisneros, and Charles Martin Wender to the five-member board. The board selected Flohr as chairman. Then they voted to file an application with the U.S. Surface Transportation Board for authority to build a new line. They authorized the staff to seek proposals for financial and rail consultants and requested startup funds from the county, which we later provided.

On Sunday the *Express-News* ran an in-depth story on West Memphis, Arkansas, which was our major competition. They had excellent surface transportation with IH-40 and IH-55 intersecting at West Memphis. They had a large Union Pacific switching yard with five railroads operating within ten miles; an international airport was ten miles away. West Memphis clearly had the best logistics for production and distribution.

The next day, Phil Wilson, Perry's communication chief, called to ask me to set up a press conference for Wednesday. The governor would travel to San Antonio to announce a grant to the rail district. I told him I would set it up in the courthouse.

Garza and several members of our legislative delegation joined the governor for the press conference in Commissioners Court chambers. Perry announced a $15 million grant to the district, noting, "The rail line is the main concern to Toyota. That's now put to rest." After the press conference I called Cuneo and left a voice mail telling him he was a master chess player. "You moved your king today, and the timing was great."

The next morning the rail grant made the front page in both Little Rock and San Antonio. The Arkansas legislature on the same day turned down Huckabee's request for a sales tax to help lure Toyota. It was a bad day for him and a good day for us.

During the Christmas holidays I turned my attention to my family and forgot about Cuneo and Toyota for a few days. The lull was short. On January 2, 2003, I received a call from Cuneo. "Things are on schedule," he said. "We've set a date. I'm not at liberty to tell you it."

"I hope it's very soon." I said. "Everyone's a bit nervous."

On January 14 Elizondo and I traveled to Austin for the opening day of the 78th Legislature. As former members, we both had floor privileges. Memories flooded me as I watched the senators draw for two- or four-year terms. Over thirty years ago on a cold and icy day, as a freshman member of the Senate, I too drew for my term. Two senators were absent, and I was the last to draw one of three remaining capsules. Two held four-year terms. I drew the one remaining two-year term. Two years later I ran for Congress instead of for reelection and lost the race. Had I drawn the four-year term, I would have remained in the Senate after I lost the congressional campaign. What might have been?

We spent the day working the floors of both the Senate and the House and were successful in gathering several votes for proposed Toyota funding.

The next Sunday Tracy and I boarded a plane for Cincinnati.

I was scheduled to meet with Cuneo at Toyota's North American corporate offices in Erlanger, Kentucky, across the river from Cincinnati. Early Monday morning my friend Jim Fonteno, a board member of the Houston Port Authority, and I drove up to a four-story brick and plate-glass building. We were escorted to an elegant room with a cherry wood conference table surrounded by eight spindle-backed chairs. The room was aptly named the Corolla, after one of Toyota's most famous automobiles. Toyota had sold more than 25 million of them, more than any other car. After greetings Fonteno assured Cuneo: "Our port will not be shut down by a union as occurred in Long Beach."

"That shutdown cost us sixty to eighty million dollars, not including lost production," Cuneo said. After Fonteno's presentation I described the rail plan and our preferred route. Cuneo said, "Looks fine to me. I'll use it to pressure Union Pacific."

After the meeting Cuneo and I went to lunch at the Metropolitan Club overlooking the Ohio River. Across the river he pointed out the recently completed Great American Ball Park, home of the Cincinnati Reds. Remnants of the old ballpark, Riverfront Stadium, are part of the complex. Next to it was the new open-roof Paul Brown Stadium where the Cincinnati Bengals play football.

"Do you think Henry Cisneros would be interested in being a partner with one of our suppliers?" Cuneo said. I promised to ask him. I did, and he was.

Over a lunch of red snapper we talked about rare and used books and home libraries. His wife was chair of the Friends of the Cincinnati Library. He had recently built a library in his home, and I was in the process of building one. Halfway through the meal Cuneo said, "Next Monday morning there will be an executive committee meeting of the Toyota board in Japan. I expect a final decision to be made. I'm optimistic."

I told him the media were pressing for more details. He said they'd probably leak the information. "That will take the pressure off you. The only thing that could delay an announcement would be if President Bush goes to war with Iraq."

The following week, as I was driving down Watson Road to the proposed entrance to the plant site, Cuneo called. "I'm going to tell Mayor Garza we don't need a nonannexation agreement or a tax abatement from the city as we originally proposed."

"Well, that's a first," I said.

"Where will you be Tuesday morning?"

"I'm planning to meet the city manager at the Toyota site. I'll have my portable phone. You may get a call."

That night, at 8:40 P.M. on January 27, Tracy came running into the bedroom where I was watching the Spurs play the Minnesota Timberwolves. "Dennis is on the phone," she said.

We went into her office, and over the speakerphone I asked, "Dennis, what happened?" He said: "We reached a major milestone. It's Tuesday morning in Japan, and Toyota's executive committee just approved the project. It still has to go to the full board, but it will likely approve it. We've scheduled the formal announcement in San Antonio on February 10. [Toyota] President Cho plans to come."

"I can't believe it's final," I said. "I really enjoyed working with you, or maybe I should say working for you."

"It's not over yet," he said. "I fell in love with your city after my first trip. But don't let your guard down. Things could still go wrong."

After we said our goodbyes, I told Tracy, "The tension in my body just slipped down to my toes. Strangely enough, I feel let down. It was an exhilarating pursuit, and now it's over. What will I do tomorrow?"

"Things can still go wrong," she said.

"That makes me feel better."

Cyndi Krier called and said, "I know you know and I know, and I have just got to talk about it." We talked for about fifteen minutes

The next day our newly elected U.S. Senator John Cornyn let the cat out of the bag by announcing that Toyota would make a decision within two weeks. The story made headlines on Wednesday. Bob Rivard, *Express-News* editor, called that day and said, "We're putting the pieces together. We may run a headline in the next couple of days that reads, 'Get ready to party. Toyota is coming.' "

"I wish you wouldn't," I told him.

"Toyota can't contain all the news until February 10," he said. "I need a quote from them."

"Send me a memo on how you think it should be handled," I said. "I'll forward it to Dennis."

The memo said, in part, that Toyota should make a controlled leak to the *Express-News* so that it could break an accurate story. Citing sources close to Toyota would be sufficient for the newspaper. I forwarded the memo to Cuneo, who called the next day. "Tell them I'll talk to Japan and seek permission to release the news when the board makes its final vote next week."

I relayed the offer to Rivard. "We'll run a story tomorrow," he said, "but we'll tone it down."

On January 31 the headline read, "Toyota—Are we there yet?" The story reported that the board would take one final vote sometime in the next week. That morning we met in San Antonio with Wiseman, Toyota's vice president of external affairs, who was pleased with the story. We spent the meeting going over the financial incentive package.

That afternoon I arranged for Rivard to meet with Cuneo on February 9, the day before the official announcement. I also arranged for Cuneo to meet with the leadership of COPS-Metro Alliance. Later I participated in a press conference with COPS-Metro leaders when they announced their support for the financial incentives to bring Toyota to San Antonio.

Cuneo called me at home on February 2. "In view of what happened over the weekend," he said, "my Japanese colleagues wonder whether we should reschedule our announcement."

Tracy was right. I should not have relaxed. "What happened?" I asked.

"The space shuttle accident," he said. "It may be a bad time to announce." The day before, the Columbia space shuttle had crashed on reentry, its pieces landing in Texas.

"No, we shouldn't postpone," I said. "NASA officials already think they know what went wrong. I believe the crash will be out of the news next week."

"Call your friend at the newspaper and let me know what he thinks."

I tried to reach Rivard and then publisher Larry Walker, but I was unsuccessful. So I called Cuneo back. "My newspaper friend said there's no doubt you should go ahead with the announcement," I said. I just had to do that.

"I just talked to the governor," Cuneo said. "He feels the same way. We'll stay on schedule. I'm going to quietly slip into town on Wednesday and go over everything. See you then."

Rivard called me back later in the day, and I told him what I had told Cuneo. He understood.

On Tuesday evening Garza and I attended the twenty-fifth anniversary of the San Antonio Local Development Company at the Old San Francisco Steak House. We were seated across from each other at dinner. Around 8:30 P.M. my phone rang, and Hernandez said, "Dennis wants to talk to you." I quickly walked from the room.

"The board just announced its decision," Cuneo said. "We'll have a press conference tomorrow morning in San Antonio. You can tell the media the decision is official and tell them about the press conference."

When I arrived home an hour later, two television crews wired for live coverage were waiting for me. The decision had already hit the AP wires. I said that indeed the decision was official.

When I arrived at the Westin Riverwalk the next morning, the room was already jam-packed with media. Legislators, commissioners, and council members were gathered around Cuneo in a side room to thank him. A beaming Governor Perry and his wife,

Anita, arrived. Democrats and Republicans hugged each other. You would have thought we were all in the same political party.

Perry led us into the packed Encino Room and opened the press conference. "San Antonio, you asked for it and you got it," he said.

I said, "As Peter Holt and the Spurs fans would say, 'Go Toyota, go.'"

The crowd greeted Cuneo with extended applause. He said what a wonderful reception San Antonio had given Toyota and noted that the financial incentive package was the lowest Toyota had received—$133 million in direct incentives that included tax abatements, land purchase, a rail district grant, job training, fee waivers, and utility infrastructure. The site would become one of three federal empowerment zones in San Antonio. That allowed Toyota to claim a tax credit for each worker residing within the zone.

After the press conference Garza and I had lunch with Toyota officials and the *Express-News* Editorial Board. Cuneo reviewed how the deal had progressed. He said the rail district and job-training funds were critical components, and without them Toyota would not have come to Texas.

Automobile experts criticized Toyota's decision in no time. An article in *Automotive News* argued that Toyota would pay a price for lengthening its U.S. supply chain. An expert was quoted as saying, "There's no question it's an odd choice in locations."

Toyota has a strong history of leadership in the auto industry. It opened the door to automobile manufacturing in the growing

Southwest. Its marketing people had prevailed over its manufacturing people.

The announcement that Toyota selected San Antonio was contingent on us following through on our promises. I testified at the Senate Finance Committee on Madla's bill to appropriate $15 million for the rail district. The bill passed from committee on a 13–0 vote. I spoke before the Texas Transportation Commission requesting funding to build interchanges at Loop 410 and Loop 1604 that connected to Applewhite Road. The commission awarded us $17.6 million.

Garza and the city council created the Starbright Industrial Development Corp. to sell bonds to pay for the $14 million purchase price of some 2,000 acres of land, $3 million for the training facility, and $10 million for site preparation. The San Antonio Water System provided Toyota with an additional 600 acres.

Toyota's sleek white jet rolled up to the tarmac at the Hallmark Institute near the San Antonio airport on March 8. Garza, Cisneros, and I watched a short elderly man with a stocky frame and a full head of white hair emerge from the jet. He was dressed in a dark blue suit, a white shirt, and a yellow tie with blue diagonal stripes. With looks and movements that belied his seventy-five years, Toyota Chairman Shoichiro Toyoda approached us with a brisk walk and gave us a firm handshake. Accompanying him were his wife, Hiroko, and Yoshimi Inaba, president of Toyota Motor Sales, USA.

We walked upstairs to a conference room and gathered around a small table. Through an interpreter Toyoda said, "Thank you for meeting with me. I apologize for the inconvenience of disturbing your Saturday. On another occasion I will come back for a formal visit. Thank you for accepting our company in such a warm way. I hope expectations have not been raised too high. We'll do our best to meet them." He invited us to the upcoming Expo fair in Nagoya, Japan, and to meet with some of Toyota's suppliers.

I presented him a copy of my book *Mayor*, which Cisneros, Garza, and I had signed. I asked him to sign my copy of the book *Against All Odds*, the story of Toyota. He leafed through its pages, smiled, and noted through the interpreter, "Here's a picture of my grandfather and father. Here I am in front of the headquarters with my cousin Eiji and a statue of my father behind us."

After a forty-five-minute conversation, we watched the Toyota officials drive off in a convoy of three black Sequoias and an Avalon.

We still had a lot of work to do to fulfill our obligation to Toyota. Back in Austin on March 17 I walked onto the House floor to be present for the final passage of the $15 million appropriation bill for the rail district. Several groups of legislators were on the floor kidding around and lobbying each other on upcoming bills. That's the way the House works. In the vast majority of cases, by the time a bill gets to the floor the outcome has been determined. So there is not much need to play close attention to what happens at the front mike. Everyone knows how to count votes beforehand.

I walked up to Reps. Robert Puente and Elizabeth Ames Jones and spun an old tale for them. I said, "I remember when former Rep. Jake Johnson [D-San Antonio], my old suitemate, presented a resolution at the front mike. The members voted it down. They knew they couldn't support it because Jake was a flaming liberal. After the vote he said, 'Fellow members, you just voted down the Bill of Rights of the United States Constitution.' "

Jones said, "We're too civil today to trick members like that."

Rep. Paul Moreno pulled up to us in his wheelchair. His House desk was next to mine when we served together in 1970. I said, "Paul, when you convinced me to vote for a resolution honoring Cesar Chavez, every one of my political opponents used it against me." He laughed and said, "You should be grateful that I made you famous."

But as Puente made his way to the mike we stopped talking and paid attention. Our local delegation gathered around him as he began to speak in favor of the $15 million appropriation. The bill passed without a dissenting vote. Puente then introduced Wiseman, who was sitting in the balcony. He received a nice round of applause.

As Wiseman and I drove back to San Antonio, I got a call from Ron Olson, Union Pacific's legislative lobbyist, to set up a dinner with Union Pacific officials. Once the bill passed they'd wasted no time.

Commissioners Court took the next steps. On March 26 we voted to establish a 2,700-acre tax reinvestment zone and approved the outline of an incentive package for Toyota suppliers. This was important because more than thirty cities in central Texas were organizing to entice Toyota suppliers to their area. A few weeks later we approved the county's ten-year tax phase-in agreement with Toyota. Commissioner Adkisson, who usually opposes tax phase-ins, called this one "the poster child for what's right about economic incentives." We also approved the 126-page comprehensive Starbright agreement, which nineteen government and private entities would have to approve and sign. Two days later I delivered the agreement to a city council meeting for approval.

During a Commissioners Court meeting on June 4, Judge Tom Rickhoff called and asked me to attend a 10 A.M. meeting at attorney Tommy Smith's office. "Some members of the Walsh family are refusing to sign the deeds," he said. "We need you to apply some pressure."

The city was committed to issuing bonds three days later to pay $13,810,352 owed to the Walsh family for some 1,700 acres it was purchasing for Toyota. Without signed deeds, no bonds could be issued, and the city could not sign the final agreement with Toyota.

The Walsh family had a history of infighting. Patricia Small and her sister, Caroline Murguia, had been feuding for eighteen years. They also battled with their mother, Mary Louise Walsh. Now, with more than $13 million about to be split up, ninety-two-year-old Momma Walsh decided to use a little leverage to settle some longstanding issues.

When we arrived for the meeting, Patricia, Caroline, and Mary Louise were sitting at a table, each with her own lawyer. Smith, the lawyer for Patricia and her husband, John Small, explained the disagreement over who should be trustees for the children of Patricia and Caroline. He suggested closing the land transaction and parking the money until the issue could be settled. Mary Louise Walsh's lawyer, Henry Amen, said they should settle the trustee issue now or she would not sign.

I pleaded with them not to use the closing to settle an eighteen-year argument. I told them we were leaving for Japan in two days, and we had to report to Toyota that the deal was closed. I explained that the city could not issue bonds unless it had a deed to the land.

Lawyers for all parties left the room to confer, and I sat down next to Mary Louise. "I love a good family brawl," she said. "I'm Irish, and I came here from Louisiana where we had some good fights."

"I hope you won't let this family fight get out of hand," I told her. "This closing is important to a lot of people."

She just smiled. She was enjoying herself.

After several hours of meetings, the family settled the trustee issue. But two nights later Smith called me at 10 P.M. "They want my client to sign an agreement giving up all rights to sue for any previous actions. My client won't sign. Can we meet with you tomorrow at the airport before you leave?"

As I was checking in, Smith arrived. "Maybe it would be good for the whole delegation to come into the meeting," he said.

I sat down between Smith and Amen, the lawyer for Mary Louise Walsh, and listened to both sides. Various members of our delegation came in and sat quietly.

"You're being very unreasonable," I told Amen. "This issue is much bigger than a family squabble. Jobs and the well-being of a lot of people are at stake. You may end up costing your client a great deal of money if Toyota decides to walk away. And they will walk away, because they do not like controversy."

"I believe we can settle this before the closing," Amen said.

"If we don't close this deal, you may have to go into the Witness Protection Program," Smith said.

After another thirty minutes of conversation, the lawyers agreed on the time and format for the closing. We rushed to get on the plane. When we arrived in Tokyo the next day, we were informed that the closing had been completed.

Cisneros, Garza, and I had club sandwiches that evening by a window framing a beautiful garden at the Hotel Okura in Tokyo. Cisneros told Garza, "Your second term is off to a successful start."

"I haven't done anything yet," Garza replied.

"That's why," I said, and laughed.

We chatted about politics for a couple of hours. The three of us had never sat down together in San Antonio—we had to go to Japan to do it.

As leader of the delegation, I chaired some fifteen meetings the next week, including a series of formal meetings with Toyota officials, several suppliers, and government leaders. We also toured the Toyota plant in Toyota City and some supplier plants near the Toyota facility. By nightfall each day, I was ready to hit the hay before my colleagues were. Our major accomplishment was an agreement to build a supplier park on site, the first of its kind at a Toyota plant in the United States.

Finally, in August Union Pacific announced that it would allow access to Burlington Northern Santa Fe Railroad on its rail line. Before Union Pacific granted it, though, we had to fund a new rail line and receive approval of the route by the U.S. Surface Transportation Board.

Shoichiro Toyoda returned to San Antonio for the formal groundbreaking ceremonies on October 17. Tracy and I joined Garza and his wife for breakfast at La Mansión del Rio, with Toyoda and his wife, Hiroko, and T.J. Tajima, president of Toyota, Texas, and his wife, Miho. Then we made our way to the site, gathering in a shielded section of a large white tent that could hold 1,000. Busloads of people from a nearby parking lot began to arrive. Excitement filled the air. This was the largest groundbreaking ceremony ever held in San Antonio.

As Toyoda, Tajima, Governor Perry, Garza, Cuneo, and I walked to the stage, a huge round of applause went up. After our short remarks, we each shoveled spades of dirt. Streamers showered the crowd, and music played. The RK Group catered a lunch using Toyota pickups as buffet tables. What a grand time we had.

Less than two months later Cuneo called, leaving me a message that he was being transferred to New York to become senior vice president of Toyota Motor North America. He would oversee governmental affairs, public relations, and investor and industry relations.

Over the next few months I met several times with Tajima to plan for the supplier park. In March 2004 he announced that at least ten suppliers would locate there, investing more than $100 million and employing at least 1,000 workers. In December he announced that the number had risen to eighteen suppliers, employing at least 1,500 people and investing $175 million. He said six minority partners, including four from San Antonio, would invest with some of the suppliers. One was Cisneros. Commissioners Court approved a tax phase-in for the suppliers, who by then had agreed to employ 2,000 workers and invest more than $300 million in buildings and equipment.

On July 27, 2005, I joined Phil Hardberger, who had been elected mayor the previous May, on a trip to Japan. In Tokyo we had lunch with the powerful Keidanren business council. That night we attended a reception at the U.S. embassy with Ambassador Tom Schieffer and his wife, Susanne. Her father, Paul Silber, and I had served together in the Texas legislature.

After a weekend trip to the historic city of Kyoto we traveled by train to Nagoya, the Expo site. Toyoda, who was chairman of the Expo, hosted us for dinner. We had a great time comparing Japanese and American baseball teams and their players. The next day we attended an evening reception for the Texas delegation at the U.S. Pavilion. Tajima pulled Hardberger and me aside to tell us that the next day Katsuaki Watanabe, the president of Toyota Motor Corp., would announce that Toyota would invest an additional $50 million and produce 50,000 more vehicles in San Antonio.

At the meeting, a smiling Cuneo was present as Watanabe told us of the increased investment. That evening Hardberger, Cisneros, and I held a press conference with the San Antonio media to announce the good news over a portable phone that we passed around.

When we arrived home Tajima announced three more suppliers, bringing the total to twenty-one. No other plant in the world has this many suppliers on site.

On February 28, 2006, San Antonio properly honored Naoko Shirane when the World Affairs Council of San Antonio named her its International Citizen of the Year. Toyoda was the keynote speaker. As co-founder of the World Affairs Council and its first chairman, I was delighted that Mrs. Shirane was recognized. In her acceptance speech she said, "I look forward to working with you the rest of my life." What a wonderful commitment.

In early November Cuneo called. "I'm retiring, moving back to Washington, and joining my old law firm," he said. "I'll continue to do work for Toyota under a consulting contract on new manufacturing locations." He had left his mark on Toyota, and his decision to select San Antonio had a major impact on our city. We had become good friends, and I was sad to see him go.

On November 17 Toyota hosted a ceremony to commemorate the first Tundra that rolled off the production line. Held on the factory floor, the celebration included all the Toyota team members. A ranch setting, centered with a barn façade fronted by a ranch gate, was created on a large stage. The sign on the gate announced the Triple T Ranch (Toyota, Tundra, and Texas). Hay, saddles, and barrels sat in front of the barn. Two large television screens towered on the sides. After all of the politicians gave two-minute speeches, President Watanabe told the crowd that the Tundra was the single most important product introduced in the last fifty years.

Tajima then took the stage to thunderous applause from his team, telling the audience that Toyota and its twenty-one suppliers had invested $1.58 billion in more than 4 million square feet of buildings and were employing more than 4,100 people. Then team members, really pumped up, rode out of the barn in two Tundras, with smoke, flashing lights, and music.

Toyota announced in February 2007 that they had received a $300 million incentive package from Mississippi to build a plant near Tupelo. Our package of $133 million proved to be very prudent. They also announced that they would not build a supplier park as they did in San Antonio.

In early March Hardberger and I met with Tajima in Hardberger's office. Tajima told us he would be leaving San Antonio to head up a major international division for the company. "I'll come back to see you," he said. In four years he had built the plant, overseen the construction of the supplier park, hired 2,200 employees, and had Tundra pickups rolling off the line. Now it was time to continue his climb up the corporate ladder. Kenji Fukuta was named to take his place.

Both T. J. Tajima and Dennis Cuneo have gone their respective ways, but their contribution to our city will not be forgotten. Toyota has come to town, and San Antonio will never be the same.

FOUR

The San Antonio River Walk Extension

ON A BEAUTIFUL SPRING DAY in May 2007, after Lou Agnese, president of the University of the Incarnate Word, and I had lunch in the historic Victorian Brackenridge Villa, we walked some 100 yards toward the northwest area of the campus. Under several large trees, we came upon an artesian well, known as the Blue Hole. Bubbling out of the well was crystal clear water that flowed to the campus footbridge, where Olmos Creek and spring water come together to form the San Antonio River. The river flows south 180 miles to join the Guadalupe River and then washes into the Gulf of Mexico.

As we looked at the Blue Hole, I told Agnese about the beautiful springs I saw bubbling out of the grounds on the northern edge of UIW during the flood of 1998. Among several oaks and palm trees, I watched a magical display of natural sprinklers spewing clear water from the Edwards Aquifer, a porous karst limestone formation stretching 185 miles across six counties. "That happens only on rare occasions," Agnese said, "but the water from our Blue Hole runs continuously except during times of severe drought."

The river also receives water from Leon, Cibolo, Olmos, and Salado creeks, as well as more than 100 underground springs. San Pedro Creek provides additional water when it merges with the river in south San Antonio at Concepción Park.

When people visit San Antonio, they see only the River Walk, the downtown section of the river lined with restaurants, hotels, and retail stores. Ever since HemisFair in 1968, the River Walk has grown in density and popularity, and significant public improvements have been made. Unfortunately the rest of the river has been neglected and abused until now. As this book goes to press, we are in the early stages of a $200 million, thirteen-mile San Antonio River Walk extension linking the headwaters north of downtown to Mission Espada south of the city. This project is perhaps the most important local public works project of our time.

The river drew Spanish explorers and then settlers to this area centuries ago. On June 13, 1691, Franciscan Father Damian Massanet came upon the Payaya Indian village of Yanaguana, located on the banks of a narrow, meandering river. He named it the San Antonio River in honor of San Antonio de Padua. Nearly twenty-seven years later, on April 25, 1718, Martín de Alarcón arrived with seventy-two Spanish settlers and soldiers, setting up a small community and a presidio, or fort, near San Pedro Springs. One month later Father Antonio Olivares arrived to establish Mission San Antonio de Valero, now called the Alamo, nearby. In 1722 the presidio was moved south to the northern edge of what became Military Plaza, where City Hall is today. In 1724 the Alamo ended up a distance of "two gunshots" east of Military Plaza, above the far bank of the San Antonio River. Following the river south,

Father Antonio Margil de Jesús founded Mission San José in 1720. In the 1730s three other missions—Espada, San Juan Capistrano, and Concepción—were built farther south along the river.

While the missions downriver were under construction, fifty-five Spanish Canary Islanders arrived on March 9, 1731. They laid out a traditional Spanish plaza and built their homes near the area that remains the historic heart of San Antonio.

The river became the lifeline for the early Spanish civilian and mission communities. Several miles south of town, native converts under the direction of Spanish priests built Espada dam to divert water into an irrigation ditch. They then built an aqueduct to carry the ditch above the slight valley of a narrow creek so the water could continue downgrade to irrigate mission farmland. The river also provided water to drink, as well as a recreation area for camping, bathing, and swimming.

In the 1840s many Germans settled in the area and recognized the river's commercial potential. They built several mills along the river. Pioneer Flour Mills, located near the King William neighborhood, remains in business today.

When Frederick Law Olmsted, architect of New York City's Central Park, visited San Antonio in 1857, he wrote: "The whole river gushes up in one sparkling burst from the earth. It has all the beautiful accompaniments of a smaller spring, moss, pebbles, seclusion, sparkling sunbeams and dense overhanging luxuriant foliage. The effect is overpowering."

With the arrival of railroads in the late 1870s, the population grew rapidly, and soon after the turn of the century San Antonio had become the largest city in Texas. Numerous artesian wells were drilled into the aquifer to meet the demands of a larger population. As a result, the water table dropped and the headwaters and several underground springs feeding the river began to dry up. The wonderful river that had attracted Olmsted's praise was fast becoming a shallow stream.

According to Lewis F. Fisher's book *River Walk: The Epic Story of San Antonio's River*, a pump installed in 1911 in Brackenridge Park immediately south of the headwaters extracted water from the aquifer and added it to the river. This augmented the river's flow as it meandered downstream. Brackenridge Park featured pavilions, ballparks, and numerous picnic sites along the river. That same year brought the first efforts toward establishing a formal park along the riverbanks, which San Antonians had been clamoring to beautify since 1904. The San Antonio River Improvement Association's efforts culminated in 1914 with the opening of the city-constructed River Park, with landscaped banks and low rock and concrete walls on the river's edge through downtown, including along the horseshoe-shaped River Bend.

The periodic flooding that caused the San Antonio River to overflow the downtown streets and banks of the bend became increasingly serious as new development caused more runoff. After two major floods in 1913, City Hall commissioned a major flood control plan, approved in 1920. The following year, however, floodwaters rose to a level not seen in more than a century. They reached some twelve feet at the downtown intersection of Houston and St. Mary's streets, and many homes in low-lying areas were swept away. More than fifty people drowned.

Implementation of the 1920 flood control plan went into high gear. Historically, the greatest source of floodwater was the drainage area of normally dry Olmos Creek. Citizens approved $2.8 million in bonds to pay for a dam in 1926 where Olmos Creek flows into the San Antonio River. Another critical problem was the downtown River Bend, which slowed floodwaters and created a serious flood hazard. Flood plan engineers had recommended removing all trees and shrubbery around the bend and paving its channel as an open culvert, a proposal that, before the flood, City Hall had rejected due to pressure from irate citizens. Instead, in 1930 a concrete-lined bypass channel was completed straight through downtown as an overflow passageway to carry floodwater past the downtown bend, which would retain its natural appearance. Gates at the end of the two bend entrances were lowered during floods, protecting the bend itself from flooding.

Once serious flooding problems had been solved, a new proposal came up on how to best develop the bend. In 1929 landscape architect Robert Hugman revealed his "Shops of Aragon and Romula" plan, which envisioned the river bend as similar to small winding landscaped streets in Spain, with shops and restaurants on its banks. City Hall, however, listened to opponents and adopted a citywide master plan that included maintaining the riverbanks in a parklike setting, established in 1914, with only trees, flowers, and grass.

A successful river parade marking the Texas Centennial in 1936 was evidence enough for Jack White, manager of a hotel along the bend, that people could be attracted to the river and that Hugman's plan for some commercial development had potential. In 1938 White helped raise local funds to match federal WPA funds supporting Hugman's plan to improve twenty-one blocks of the bend. Hugman was hired to oversee the project's construction, with sidewalks of flagstone, brick, and concrete; thirty-one stairways to the street level; and landscaping that included 11,000 trees. Although conservationists who preferred that the river remain strictly a park were successful in getting Hugman fired after one year, the project proceeded and was completed in 1941.

This was the river I remember as a young boy growing up in San Antonio. In the late 1940s my mother, my brother George, and I would catch a bus downtown. While my mother shopped, George and I went to the movies at the Majestic Theatre. Then Mother took us to play along the bend. Sometimes we stopped to eat Mexican food at Casa Rio, which was built on the bend in 1946. This was the only business there at the time.

In 1962 businessman David Straus, voicing the concerns of many San Antonians about the deserted River Walk, successfully presented an ordinance to the City Council establishing a River Walk district and a seven-member River Walk Advisory Commission. That same year the city's parks department planted 17,000 trees, as well as shrubs, vines, and groundcover. During this time I attended St. Mary's School of Law, then located on the bend. When I graduated in 1966 we had a big party at The Landing, in the basement of the nearby Nix Hospital. Straus and fellow businessman James Haynes had persuaded Jim Cullum to open the jazz club in 1963. After drinking and listening to great jazz all night, we closed up the place, went outside, and jumped into the river fully clothed to celebrate our graduation.

In 1968 the river was extended east to connect with the newly constructed convention center, which had been built on the ninety-two-acre HemisFair grounds. Flat-bottom steel-hulled barges were now the mode of river transportation. The connection to the convention center provided incentive for hotels to be built on the bend. I watched Zachry Construction Corp. use a crane to stack 481 modular rooms that would make up the Hilton Palacio del Rio. I observed Pat Kennedy renovate the 1852 St. Mary's Law School building into the 200-room La Mansión del Rio. The tranquility of the river that we experienced as law students was quickly passing.

In the 1980s the U.S. Army Corps of Engineers completed a river beautification project from downtown Nueva Street south to Arsenal Street. This is the spectacular section of the river that runs beside the King William neighborhood. The San Antonio River Authority's headquarters, built in 1975, is located across the river from the neighborhood. At Nueva Street, the city and county built a new marina, dam, and bridge. The dam kept the upstream River Walk at a constant level. With the completion of this extension, the River Walk continued some three miles south from Lexington Avenue to Arsenal Street.

During the 1980s and 1990s intensive development occurred along this three-mile stretch, in particular in the bend area. In 1981 the 633-room Hyatt Regency San Antonio was built with a water link to Alamo Plaza. Charles Butt, CEO of the H.E. Butt Grocery Co., built the company headquarters on the river across from the King William neighborhood in 1985. He chose ten acres of land that had been the U.S. Army Arsenal, a munitions depot operating from 1859 to 1949. He restored several historic buildings on the site, creating one of the country's most innovative corporate campuses. In 1987, as a freshman member of the city council, I attended the grand opening of the 1,000-room San Antonio Marriott Rivercenter, a hotel adjacent to Rivercenter shopping mall. The river had been extended yet again to the mall and hotel.

By the time I became mayor in 1991, many other river projects were on the drawing board. To emphasize the river's importance to the city, I chose the historic Arneson River Theater, built in 1941, as the setting for my city council colleagues and me to be sworn in. The outdoor theater with its curving tiers of concrete seats extends down to the water from an arched gate that leads to La Villita. Across the narrow river bend, on the theater's small stage, we took our oath of office. Thirteen years earlier Mayor Lila Cockrell had joined Robert Hugman at the same location to dedicate five bells hung in the open arches behind the stage to honor him. The swearing-in ceremony was symbolic of the council's commitment to further develop and improve the river. During my four years as mayor, the council undertook a number of important and highly visible river initiatives.

In September 1993 the city, with the Army Corps of Engineers, broke ground on a three-mile underground tunnel that drew in runoff near Josephine Street north of downtown and released it south of the central city at Lone Star Boulevard. This would force floodwaters under the downtown area. The project included a recirculation feature at the Lone Star outlet to allow water to be reused in the river. No longer would the three wells in Brackenridge Park have to pump aquifer water into the river, and no longer would the river outside the bend flood. The tunnel would also allow building closer to the river. The project was completed in December 1997.

The city also authorized funding and completed a design for doubling the size of the city's convention center. The design included a river extension to HemisFair Park's Plaza Mexico, under a glass-enclosed hallway that bridged the two main convention center areas.

In December 1993 I traveled down the bend on a barge with Steven Tyler, lead singer for Aerosmith, and several dignitaries. Tyler sang a song for me on the way to the groundbreaking of Tim Hixon's 50,000 square-foot South Bank complex, which would house the Hard Rock Cafe.

In another major project, the city tunneled under Crockett Street, connecting the river to four buildings that backed up on the street and giving them river entrances. This involved reconstructing one block of Crockett that ran along the south side of the river across from La Mansión del Rio. In 1995 we celebrated the opening of the first phase, attorney Pat Maloney's 50,000 square-foot Presidio complex. Hotelier Pat Kennedy's Watermark Hotel and Spa opened in 2004, and Aztec on the River, a building that includes the historic Aztec Theater, opened in 2006.

Closer to City Hall, we developed and approved a Historic Civic Center Master Plan targeting the area between the river and Market Square, located a few blocks west. The idea was to revive the city's historic civic center by tying it to the river and improving the area's infrastructure and buildings. We accomplished several aspects of the plan before I left office. We built new city council chambers in the Municipal Plaza Building that faces Main Plaza. We closed Treviño Street between San Fernando Cathedral and the Municipal Plaza Building, turning it into a plaza. We restored

City Hall's exterior. We bought the Alameda Theater and created a foundation, chaired by Henry Muñoz, to restore it. We restored Milam Park across from Market Square, and we bought a parking lot on the river's west bank across from Main Plaza. The purchase was aimed at creating a park linking the river to the historic civic center.

As projects along the river progressed, we realized that continued intense development could lead to overcrowding on the River Walk. If we did not improve additional sections of the river and expand the River Walk, we would kill our greatest tourist attraction. But if we could improve the river from near its headwaters to Mission Espada, we could create a pleasant natural environment for both citizens and tourists. This thirteen-mile section of the river, with walking and hiking trails, could connect north and south San Antonio in a way that all our citizens would enjoy.

The idea of the River Walk extension began in 1988 during my second year on the city council. The county, city, and the San Antonio River Authority (SARA) authorized two studies to develop a conceptual plan for the river. SARA was created in 1937 by the Texas legislature. Its twelve board members are elected from Bexar, Wilson, Karnes, and Goliad counties. SARA's responsibilities include flood control, river maintenance, water quality, and environmental services and river-related recreation for the entire length of the 240-mile river. In Bexar County SARA serves as the local sponsor of the Army Corps of Engineers on various flood control projects and coordinates the federal agency's involvement.

In March 1993, during the second year of my mayoral term,

the city council adopted the conceptual plan for the river from Guenther Street in the King William area south to Espada Dam. In December we adopted a conceptual plan for the river from downtown Nueva Street north to U.S. 281. To complement the thirteen-mile plan, we began work on the Mission Trails project, which would provide trails from the Alamo through ten miles of the southern city, connecting with the other four missions. One part of the route, along the river, included hike-and-bike trails, landscaping, and picnic areas.

Howard Peak, then a councilman and later mayor, took the lead in advocating the project. Working in the city's Planning Department for a decade and serving on the Planning Commission for four years, he was well trained for the task. To get a firsthand view of the proposed project, he ventured north on the river, crawling through what he described as a mud ditch. As he made his way through weeds and trash, he looked up at the backs of buildings along the river. He also walked down the banks of the southern river extension to view the 1960 work of the Army Corps of Engineers. The corps had straightened the river, built concrete embankments in some places, denuded trees lining the banks, installed boulders and riprap, and added loose stones to the water and nearby soft ground. The corps' misguided work, aided by neglect, had done horrible environmental damage to our most precious resource.

After I was term limited out of office in 1995, the city council funded the design of the proposed river park entrance on Main Plaza, to be located on the parking lot we had purchased earlier. During Mayor Bill Thornton's term, preliminary engineering work on the plan proceeded. When Peak became mayor in 1997, he led a successful bond campaign to pay for the entrance. He also convinced the city council to fund a Houston Street linkage to the river. That project included a new stairway to the river on Presa Street one block south of Houston Street. In response to the project, Federal Realty Investment Trust put more than $100 million into Houston Street properties.

After preliminary engineering plans for the River Walk extension were completed in September 1997, Peak began pulling people together to find a way to pay for it. He met with Commissioner Mike Novak and SARA board member Clifton McNeel to propose a tri-party plan. Years later, when I talked with Novak, he recalled:

> When I was a student at St. Mary's University, Father Louis Reile wrote a book titled *Winding Flows the River*. I became fascinated with the story of the San Antonio River. I would read excerpts from the book at public hearings when I promoted the improvement of the river. I ran into trouble with Commissioner Robert Tejeda when I first presented it to Commissioners Court. He said he would kill the proposal unless he had assurance that the southern section would be funded at the same time as the north section. When I promised him it would be, he became supportive. I believe the river not only reflects our history; it also reflects the essence and soul of our community. The city and county need to make sure this project is finished.

In spring 1998, the city, county, and SARA formed a Committee of Six that included two representatives from each entity to guide the river improvements. The Committee of Six created the San Antonio River Oversight Committee. The twenty-two-member committee, co-chaired by former mayor Lila Cockrell and architect Irby Hightower, was charged with overseeing planning, design, project management, and funding.

The following year the county and city were in a major conflict over the right to build a new arena for the Spurs. Although tensions were high, County Judge Cyndi Krier and Mayor Peak continued working together on the river. On May 4, 1999, Krier led the effort on Commissioners Court to commit up to $73 million in county flood control funds to the river project. The project got a significant boost in November 2000 when Congress passed legislation authorizing the Army Corps of Engineers to add ecosystem restoration and recreation to the project, allowing congressional funding to repair damage to the river environment that the corps had caused in the 1960s.

With county funding in place, Peak sought voter approval for the city's contribution. The city council submitted four propositions on a May 6 ballot, one of which would increase the sales tax to pay for river improvements. Unfortunately the river proposal failed.

Before Peak was term limited out of office in May, he persuaded the city council to commit $37 million to the project. But the commitment did not identify a funding source, and the next council was not required to provide funding. There was adequate funding for the one-mile Downtown Reach, and construction began before Peak and Krier left office.

Krier resigned as county judge the same month Peak's term was up. Ed Garza succeeded him, and Commissioners Court appointed me to succeed Krier. No sooner had we both taken office than we were greeted with bad news. The Goldsbury Foundation and the Kronkosky Charitable Foundation withdrew private-sector commitments of $10 million. We tried to revive the funding, but the two foundations would not reconsider.

With the loss of private funding, questionable funding from the city, and the Army Corps of Engineers funding subject to annual congressional appropriations, the project was in trouble. The only available funding was for the one-mile Downtown Reach and one mile just south of downtown. For the remaining eleven miles only the county had identified funding, which we set aside from our flood control tax.

We did have a plan, however. Two months after I took office the project's concept design was completed. The estimated cost was $140.7 million. Bexar County would contribute $53.6 million; the city, $37.8 million; the Army Corps of Engineers, $34.3 million; and the private sector, $15 million.

The river plan was divided into three major segments. The Mission Reach extended south nine miles from downtown Alamo Street to Mission Espada. This section of the river flows from downtown past Brackenridge High School, Roosevelt Park, Mission Concepción, Riverside Golf Course, Mission San José, Mission County Park, over the historic San Juan and Espada dams, past Acequia Park and Mission San Juan, and finally to Mission Espada. The improvements would restore ecosystems and improve habitats for birds, fish, and wildlife. The project would also reestablish historic and cultural connections between the river and the four historic missions. A linear park would set the framework for urban development with a continuous pedestrian link to adjacent urban areas.

The Museum Reach extended north four miles from Lexington Avenue to Hildebrand Avenue on the northern edge of Brackenridge Park. This part of the river flows by the San Antonio Zoo, the historic Pearl Brewery, the Witte Museum, the San Antonio Museum of Art, and the park. A lock near Brooklyn Street would allow barges to travel upriver to a turning basin at the Pearl Brewery site. This stretch of the river offered the best opportunity for economic development. The area is a mixture of residential, commercial, and light industrial.

As we worked on the project, other developments on the downtown stretch of river continued. Five major projects were developed during Garza's two terms and my first four years as county judge.

On a sunny Sunday afternoon in October 2001, Tracy and I walked across Main Plaza toward the new park entrance to the river. Lake-Flato Architects brought together artist Celia Muñoz, landscape architects Rosa Finsley and John Ahrens, and a team of artisans, contractors, and suppliers to design the entrance. We walked down a stairway of rough-hewn limestone flanked by lush landscaping. The architects, artists, and designers had created six water features to show the various uses of river water. They had carved inscriptions into the limestone explaining the river's history.

We joined Garza and several other dignitaries to wait for

Father David Garcia and his San Fernando Cathedral parishioners. We could hear the music of mariachis as they approached the park and descended the stairs. Several of us made speeches praising the entrance's virtues. Mike Greenberg, *San Antonio Express-News* senior critic, later described the park as "a place of extraordinary delight, at once a contemplative evocation of nature and history and a vibrant urban space." The opening had been a long time coming—some nine years, covering the terms of four mayors, since we bought the parking lot in 1992.

With the park entrance completed, Garza began work on a plan to restore and expand Main Plaza, which had undergone several changes over the years. In the 1880s the plaza had been improved with sidewalks and landscaping. From 1960 to 1962 Dolorosa Street, in front of the Bexar County Courthouse, was realigned to cut through the south end of the park, leaving part of the plaza as the courthouse's front yard. The plaza was redesigned to include an oversized fountain and parking spaces on the east and west sides.

The city again hired Lake-Flato Architects, and in May 2003 the $8.77 million plan was completed. It called for enlarging the plaza and the front yard of the courthouse by taking in part of Soledad Street and Main Avenue but keeping both streets open. It also provided for stone paving on streets and sidewalks, a new interactive central fountain, landscaping, eighty-nine new trees, lighting, and new gravel paths. But Garza was unable to convince the council to proceed with construction. The plaza would wait for the next mayor, who would bring a much broader vision of the renovation. We will get to that story in a few minutes.

Meanwhile Baron Theodore Bracht, who sold the city the

parking lot for the river park entrance, reemerged to play another critical role in the River Walk's development. The baron traveled annually from his home in Schoten, Belgium, to hunt in South Texas, spending his first day in San Antonio. A wealthy man with large farming operations in New Guinea, Indonesia, Vietnam, Argentina, and Africa, he sold palm oil, tea, rubber, and bananas around the world. In San Antonio he enjoyed walking downtown in search of possible investments.

During one of his visits Baron Bracht purchased the twenty-four-story Alamo National Bank Building, which had been constructed in 1929 across the river from what had become the park entrance. After I became county judge in 2001, we became reacquainted and visited on his annual trips. On one such visit, he said, "Why hasn't someone done something with the Aztec building and its beautiful theater?"

"You should buy it and restore it," I told him.

The Aztec building, built in 1925 to recreate an ancient Aztec temple, is on Navarro Street between Crockett and Commerce streets. The theater contained replicas of Atlantean columns from the Temple of Warriors at Chichén Itzá and reproductions of pillars of the Hall of Columns in Mitla near Oaxaca. It also had replications of jaguar heads, the Quetzalcoatl serpent, funerary urns, and many other artifacts. Originally used for vaudeville acts, it later became a movie theater. Over the years the building and its theater fell into disrepair. In 1989 the San Antonio Conservation Society bought it to protect it from possible demolition.

Finally the baron could not resist the temptation. He bought the building from the Conservation Society in 1998. The Aztec building was located catty-corner from the Alamo National Bank building, which he also owned. Both had access to the river. One was on the channel bypass and the other on the River Bend.

In spring 2004 my son Kevin, who would be elected to city council the next year, walked into my office with his friend Rick Drury. Drury had on a multicolored shirt with a clashing tie. Sprouting a scruffy goatee, he did not look the part of a wealthy, successful businessman. He and his wife, Rebecca, had lived quietly in San Antonio for several years. They played together in a band, devoted themselves to their family, and ignored the social set. Drury and his family owned more than 100 Drury Inns across the nation and were the second-largest hotel chain in San Antonio. They also knew how to turn historic buildings into hotels, having already converted the downtown Petroleum Commerce Building on the San Antonio River.

After greetings, Drury said: "My family would like to do two projects on the river. We want to purchase the Alamo National Bank building from Baron Bracht and convert it into a 320-room hotel. We'll extend the River Walk around our building to connect with the walks that end at the cutoff channel gates. We'd also like to partner with the baron to restore the Aztec building and create an opening to the river under Crocket Street.

"But we have a problem with the city," he added. "They've continued to delay our application to use up to $40 million of the low-interest empowerment zone bonds. The city wants to reserve all the bond money for the proposed new convention hotel. We need your help."

The Department of Housing and Urban Development guarantees empowerment zone bonds, saving a developer about 1 percent on the interest rate. To qualify, a project must be located in the inner city and employ people who live in the area. The city had authority to approve up to $130 million in bonds at no risk to itself.

"I'll make some calls," I said. "In the meantime let's put a little pressure on the city. Send us a financial package, and we'll see what the county can do."

Commissioners Court voted to instruct our staff and our financial advisers to put together a financial plan for the project. The pressure worked. Less than six weeks later, on June 24, city council approved the use of empowerment bonds. With the funds the Drury family paid Baron Bracht for the bank building, he restored the Aztec building and theater, contracting with the Drury family to do the work.

On the night of February 25, 2006, Tracy and I attended the opening of the Aztec on the River. Baron Bracht brought his wife, Beatrice, and his three daughters, Priscilla, Theodora, and Victoria. We arrived early to tour the theater with the baron, and he showed us details of the intricate restoration. We walked downstairs where several shops and a restaurant under construction would open to the river under the Crockett Street project that had been built while I was mayor. The baron had preserved a great historic treasure for our city and provided another important link to the river.

The restoration and remodeling of the Alamo National Bank building into a hotel and the new sidewalks on the River Walk were completed in early 2007.

While work on these two projects was progressing, in 2002 businessman Kit Goldsbury purchased the twenty-three-acre Pearl Brewery site located on the northern edge of downtown. The site is on the river's Museum Reach. The brewery, which opened in 1881, was owned and operated by the Koehler family for some eighty-two years. Otto Koehler ran the brewery until he died in 1914, followed by his widow, Emma, until she died in 1943. Their nephew, Otto Andrew Koehler, ran it until he died in 1969. The brewery struggled to survive the leadership of various managers until it finally closed in 2001.

I had my first opportunity to talk with Goldsbury about his project on March 5, 2005, when he and his wife, Angela, joined Tracy and me at a Hildalgo Foundation function at the court-house. The Hildalgo Foundation, which Tracy founded and chaired, raised funds to restore the courthouse and build a children's court. Kit and Angela, through their foundation, had made a significant donation. That evening Goldsbury invited Tracy and me to tour the Pearl Brewery.

A few weeks later at the brewery he showed us their plans. "We want to build a European-style urban village that will include gardens and plazas surrounded by performing arts venues, restaurants, education institutions, and seven hundred residential living units."

As we toured the site, we saw work progressing on various projects. A construction crew was converting the oval-shaped Jersey Lilly, where I had attended numerous functions, into a state-of-the-art event space. We toured the five-story Gothic tower building that would eventually be renovated into condos. We visited the brewery shed, which was being converted into a home for the Center for Foods of the Americas, developed in consultation with the Culinary Institute of America to feature training in Latin cuisine. The brewery garage, built in 1939, would house a school run by the Aveda Institute, which develops environmentally friendly beauty products.

When they showed us a drainage problem and I offered to try to persuade the city to cure it, Goldsbury laughed and said, "If you're successful, we'll name it Nelson's Ditch." By 2006 the Center for Foods of the Americas, the Aveda Institute, and the Jersey Lilly, renamed the Pearl Stable, were open. The city had taken care of the drainage problem. Goldsbury was on his way to creating a vibrant urban village on the riverbank.

The fifth major project on the river was at the southern edge of downtown. On May 1, 2003, Garza and I attended a groundbreaking for La Cascada, an upscale high-rise condominium on the river. My friend Mitch Meyer, who once rented a warehouse to our former family business, Sun Harvest, was the developer. It is located on Dwyer Avenue just past the dam site at Nueva Street. The two-phase, twelve-story condominiums would have forty-six units offering a beautiful view of the river.

Two other hotels also opened on the bend. Goldsbury and Tim Hixon were the lead partners in building the 513-room Westin Riverwalk in 2002 and the 265-room Hotel Contessa in 2005.

The Pearl Brewery project, La Cascada condos, the Aztec building, the river park entrance, and the new Drury Hotel would have a significant impact on development along the river.

On October 14, 2002, at a press conference on the river, we

celebrated completion of the River Walk extension's first phase, the Downtown Reach from Houston Street to Lexington Avenue. Rock walls along the river were reinforced, along with additional access ramps, more lighting, enhanced landscaping, and more walkways. The artwork of Oscar Alvarado, Carlos Cortes, and Maxwell Studios added an extra touch. The $12.2 million project was completed four months early and $500,000 under budget.

This section of the river is beautiful and tranquil, and I walk it often during the noon hour. I enter at the park entrance on Main Plaza and walk past the 325-room Holiday Inn Riverwalk, opened in 1987; the 265-room Hotel Valencia, 2003; and the Left Bank Condominiums, 1979, across the river from the Southwest School of Art and Craft in the restored Old Ursuline Academy. Then I go by Municipal Auditorium and, finally, El Tropicano Riverwalk, now a Holiday Inn. It opened in 1962, the first hotel to locate on the River Walk.

On January 7, 2004, Garza and I kicked off construction of the $8.2 million Eagleland segment of the Mission Reach that encompassed a mile from Guenther Street to Lone Star Boulevard. The concrete channel was to be removed and the banks restored to a more natural setting. A rock-and-riffle, waterfall-type structure would be built. Native grasses, flowers, and bald cypress trees would be planted on the riverbanks, with hike-and-bike trails snaking alongside them.

Completing the Downtown Reach and beginning the Eagleland segment of the Mission Reach was a good start, but that did not mean the long path ahead would be smooth. In April 2004 the Army Corps of Engineers released its national environmental restoration plan, stating that it was interested in participating only in the Mission Reach segment. In fall 2004 the corps completed its assessment of the Mission Reach and announced that its cost had jumped from $34.3 million to $66.4 million. That meant we would have to intensify our lobbying effort for more federal funds.

In May 2005, when Garza was term limited out of office, my friend Phil Hardberger, a former Fourth Court of Appeals chief justice, was elected mayor. Quickly grabbing the reins of power, he targeted the River Walk extension as his top priority. Two old friends began running fast to keep up with each other.

Two months after Hardberger was elected we received more discouraging news about the river project. Technical staff from the city, county, and SARA reevaluated the Army Corps of Engineers' 2004 projected cost of $66.4 million for the Mission Reach and determined that it would rise to $73.9 million. Some thought the corps' increased funding needs were not a problem because federal money seems to flow faster than water downhill. But federal funding would prove difficult as we continued to lobby Congress.

In addition to his enthusiasm about the River Walk extension, Hardberger had something else in mind. I was surprised when he dipped his toe into the river and came up with a new concept for linking Main Plaza to the river. In early November, after a meeting in City Hall's media conference room, he told me, "I'd like to close all the streets around Main Plaza and create a park like the great plazas I've seen in Mexico."

"Close all four streets? What a great idea. Let's do it," I replied.

"I always like your positive attitude."

I was excited about Hardberger's idea because so few people

used the river park across from the plaza. Closing Soledad Street and tying the plaza to the park would create an inviting environment that could entice people up. From the plaza they could walk all the way to Market Square. Hardberger's idea greatly expanded Garza's plan.

Walking back to the courthouse after the meeting, I watched tons of cars go by as I waited at the traffic light on Dolorosa Street. I realized I should have been more cautious in my response to Hardberger. Dolorosa runs east-west on the south end of the park, as does Commerce Street on the north end. Those two streets carry about four times more vehicles than do the north-south streets of Soledad and Main Avenue.

Closing all four streets would anger motorists and create a hell of a traffic jam. By the time I reached my office I was convinced Hardberger was not serious about closing all four streets. I knew he had a good lawyer brain. Perhaps by suggesting four closures, he would settle for two. Then again, maybe not.

Later Hardberger asked his friend and landscape architect Larry Clark to sketch some drawings of the proposed plaza. He instructed Tom Wendorf, public works director, to begin a traffic study. On November 24 Greg Jefferson, a staff writer for the *Express-News*, broke a front page story about the plan. Hardberger was quoted as saying, "I wanted to bring back the Spanish concept of a place for people to gather." Ben Brewer, president of the Downtown Alliance, said downtown business owners were extremely concerned about traffic flow.

The day after the article appeared, banker Tom Frost left me a voice message saying he wanted Commissioners Court to oppose closing any of the streets. Frost Bank is north of the plaza across from the Municipal Plaza Building. Frost is a highly respected community leader who has devoted his time and energy to improving the city. As any smart politician would do when he disagrees with someone, I delayed the return call. I wanted to wait until I could get a better sense of whether Hardberger was going to run us off a cliff by pushing to close all four streets.

At our next weekly meeting I suggested to Hardberger that he keep Commerce Street open. I said it also might satisfy Frost. "Maybe it will, but I don't want to take Commerce off the table yet," he said. The following week I met with Frost in my office and told him I wasn't sure what Hardberger would do. "He may decide not to close Commerce," I said. "I don't believe closing Main and Soledad will cause any major disruption of traffic."

"Leaving Commerce open isn't a good compromise," Frost said. "We don't support closing any of the streets permanently. We'll support temporary closures for special events. Our bank will continue to oppose the plan." His stance was reinforced by Don Frost, northeast regional president of Frost Bank. In a November 25 letter to me and other public officials, he wrote, "The management team at Frost Bank is opposed to permanently closing the streets bordering Main Plaza."

I spoke before the city council five days later. I said that traffic disruption was a small price to pay for the redeveloped plaza, and that I would try to persuade Commissioners Court to contribute 25 percent of the estimated $10 million cost for the park project.

Through Christmas and the early part of 2006, the issue faded from public debate. It reignited on March 5 when architect Steve

Tillotson was quoted in the *Express-News* as saying: "I can't agree with the decision to close any of the streets. These streets have carried traffic for 275 years." A survey by the Downtown Alliance found that half those surveyed believed no streets should be closed, and only 25 percent supported closing the two north-south streets—Main and Soledad.

Hardberger told me the next day: "I'm working with Frost to reach a compromise. I'll give up on closing Commerce but not Dolorosa." He presented his plan before Commissioners Court. I had spent the previous weekend calling the commissioners and asking them to be positive. The presentation went well, although I could not convince Commissioner Tommy Adkisson, who remained opposed to closing any streets.

In May Public Works Director Wendorf released his traffic study, which found that closing Main and Soledad would have minimal impact on traffic but that closing any lanes on Commerce or Dolorosa would have a negative impact. He did not comment on the full closure of Commerce or Dolorosa, leaving the clear impression it was a bad idea.

After the study's release Hardberger called to tell me he had decided to leave the two streets open. "Good idea," I said. "This will make it easier for me to convince the court to fund the $2.5 million."

The following Wednesday, at a press conference on the front steps of City Hall, I joined Hardberger, several council members, and a number of business leaders to announce that we backed Hardberger's compromise. During the press conference I received a call from Seth Mitchell, my chief of staff, who said Adkisson was circulating a memo to commissioners to oppose all closures. He had Commissioner Sergio "Chico" Rodriguez's signature on the memo, and he was trying to get Commissioners Paul Elizondo and Lyle Larson to sign it. I hustled over to the courthouse and persuaded them not to. I barely nipped that little problem in time.

The support of VIA, our mass transit authority, would be critical to passage of Hardberger's plan. On May 24 I joined VIA Chairman Tim Tuggey on a bus ride from downtown to the South Side to promote bus ridership. As we rode, Tuggey said, "Our board passed a resolution supporting the closing of Main and Soledad, provided that the city pay for the cost of relocating bus stops to Flores Street and for the update of the West Side multimodal study [a bus transfer station that would be connected to other modes of transportation]."

The next day Downtown Alliance president Brewer told me, "We'll support closure of Main and Soledad if the council will agree to complete the 1993 Historic Civic Center Master Plan and hire an independent group to manage the plaza and build a suspension bridge over the river to the River Walk."

"I agree with all your proposals," I told him. "I believe Phil will support your ideas."

I appeared at city council on June 8 to testify for passage of the plaza plan closing Main and Soledad. When I arrived my son Kevin told me the vote would be 9–2. He was correct. Council members Roger Flores and Patti Radle voted against the plan. It was ironic that Adkisson and Flores, the commissioner and councilman who represented downtown, opposed it.

When we passed the annual county budget in September, I

made sure $2.5 million appeared in the budget for our share of the plaza.

The day before the Historic Design Review Commission met to vote on the plan, Hardberger called to say that the opposition was trying to persuade the King William neighborhood and the Conservation Society to fight it.

At the hearing on September 20, most of those testifying spoke against it. Jon Thompson, an architecture professor at the University of Texas at San Antonio, said the plan would "cripple San Antonio for the foreseeable future.... A lawn in the middle of San Antonio—are they kidding?" Poet Naomi Shihab Nye, who lives in King William, testified that closing the streets would not make the center of town livelier. Virginia Nicholas, president of the Conservation Society, said the group would rather have the streets narrowed than closed.

Even in face of this opposition, the commission voted 12–1 to approve the plan. Hardberger had done his homework with commission members ahead of time. The next day he was quoted as saying, "I learned a long time ago that if you must overcome all objections, then nothing will ever be accomplished."

The following Thursday the city council voted to spend $350,000 to move the bus stops from Main Avenue and Soledad Street to Flores Street. On Sunday *Express-News* columnist Roddy Stinson wrote that buried in the agreement between the city and VIA was a provision that VIA would pay $500,000 for two public toilets. He wrote, "It wasn't enough for Pharaoh Phil Hardberger and kowtowing council allies to cram the vagrant-attracting project down the throats of protesting bus riders, business owners, downtown residents and city taxpayers." Politics is such fun.

Wendorf presented the plaza plan to Commissioners Court. It included our demand that part of the funding be allocated to repair a storm drainage problem that led to periodic flooding in the courthouse basement. We approved the plan and $2.5 million in county funding. Adkisson, though he did not support closing the streets, voted for the funding.

The city had hired Lake-Flato Architects to design the park. Hardberger showed me updated plans that called for keeping the demarcation of Soledad Street and Main Avenue, paving them with stone, and designating them as promenades. I laughed and said, "Sounds to me like a post-Hardberger plan." He looked at me and said nothing. He did not like my little joke, but he knew what I meant. One of his successors could convert them back to streets.

At a press conference on Main Plaza, Hardberger announced that $2.8 million in private funds had been pledged for the project. Business leaders Charles Butt, Pat Kennedy, Dennis Nixon, Dolph Briscoe, Bob Davis, Lowry and Mark Mays, Red McCombs, Bruce Smith, Graham Weston, Bill Klesse, Bill Greehey, Ed Whitacre Jr., and Bartell Zachry had stepped up to the plate. We both thanked them. With $5 million from the city, $2.5 million from the county, and $2.8 million from the private sector, funding was in place. Hardberger had done a great job raising the money.

I met with architect Ted Flato and city and county staff to review the detailed plans. The front yard of the courthouse, actually part of the plaza, would be expanded east and west onto two lanes of Soledad and Main. Additional trees would be planted, with the restored 1892 fountain featuring a series of sculptures with Lady Justice on top. My wife, Tracy, had raised money for restoration of the courthouse and sculpture, which had been discovered in disrepair in a San Antonio Water System warehouse. Ron and Karen Herrmann made the donation for Lady Justice's restoration. Sculptor Gilbert Barrera was retained to do the restoration. Outdoor lighting also would highlight the courthouse.

Trees would be planted in Main Plaza, surrounded by landscaping. The limestone promenades on Soledad and Main would extend around the park on the edge of Commerce and Dolorosa. The park would be linked to the river park entrance with a water feature and stone stairway. Permanent seating would be supplemented with portable furniture. Char Miller, a professor of urban studies at Trinity University, collected historical quotations about the plaza that would be etched into the walls and paving strips. Two food kiosks and a public restroom would be built, and accent lighting would be installed in the trees.

The most outstanding feature would be five ground-level fountains arranged in vertical rows with slender jets rising anywhere from six inches to ten feet. They would be internally illuminated and programmed for demonstrations. Bruce Bugg, president of the Tobin Endowment, committed the foundation to provide a $2 million grant for the fountains.

While we were having fun with the plaza controversy, we began to worry over serious financial problems with the River Walk extension. Although we had some success with federal funding for the Mission Reach, the bulk of federal resources were proving to be elusive. We had received federal funds to pay for the studies and design, but no construction money.

In March 2006 I traveled with SARA General Manager Greg Rothe and Assistant General Manager Suzanne Scott to Washington, D.C., to meet with officials from the Office of Management and Budget and from the Army Corps of Engineers. Neither group demonstrated any commitment for the project. We then met with members of our congressional delegation, who offered hope for funding.

After Hardberger traveled to D.C. the next month, he publicly expressed frustration with Congressman Henry Bonilla, a member of the Appropriations Committee, who would not support our $17 million river budget request. Bonilla defended his record by pointing out that he had pushed for $11 million for the project over the previous five years. After all our efforts, we received $4 million in the 2007 budget.

But receiving only partial funding did not stop us from making announcements. On September 7 John Paul Woodley Jr., assistant secretary of the Army for Civil Works, announced that 30 percent of the design of the Mission Reach was complete and that construction would start the following summer, assuming funding was provided.

While the southern Mission Reach was in a financial ditch, I began talking with fellow court members about how the county could find money for the project. We had two options. We could raise our flood control tax, or we could use the hotel-motel tax as a funding source. Or perhaps we could use both sources. We began to develop various financial proposals.

Meanwhile Hardberger was becoming frustrated with the pace of the Museum Reach, which included the two-mile urban section and the two-mile park section. In mid-August we met at El Mirador restaurant with representatives from SARA. Hardberger told Rothe and chairman Louis Rowe that he wanted the project started as soon as possible, and he wanted the urban section completed within twenty-four months from its start. He also said he wanted to hire a private firm to oversee construction. Under our three-party agreement, SARA was responsible for overseeing the construction. Rothe responded that the project was on time and that it was their responsibility to manage it.

I have had my frustrations with SARA over the years, but I was concerned that we were getting too many cooks in the kitchen. I expressed my reservations to Hardberger and suggested that if the city wanted another cook it should hire one to represent the city. The city hired PBS&J, an engineering consulting firm, as their oversight consultant.

As we drew closer to putting the project out for bid, SARA reestimated the cost based on the now completed plans. The county's cost increased by $5 million and city's by $9 million. In addition, the city had to face the fact that it had raised only $3 million—from Kit Goldsbury, owner of the Pearl Brewery site—out of the planned $10 million in private-sector contributions for the urban section. The city had to make up the $7 million shortfall.

In September Commissioners Court approved an additional $5.3 million, and in October city council approved an additional $16.6 million, which included the $7 million shortfall from the private sector. The total urban section budget was now $39 million. Construction was expected to start in December.

The bid proposal included a twenty-four-month construction timeline, along with numerous other onerous requirements of the contractor. On December 21, while the bid was on the street, an estimate of the project's cost, based on the new bid requirements, was completed. The city recommended the firm of AG/CM to do the reestimate; it found that the project's cost would be approximately $47 million rather than $39 million.

We received only one bid. Zachry Construction Corp. bid $59 million and listed 113 exceptions. We were now in a fine mess. We had received an unresponsive bid that was $20 million over our budgeted funds. Commissioners thought we should reject it and rebid the package under different terms. But the city wanted a chance to negotiate with Zachry. We agreed to give it a chance. City Manager Sheryl Sculley led a team of county, city, and SARA officials in negotiations with Zachry.

While shock at the project's rising cost caught us staring like deer in the headlights, we got a bit of good news. On the evening of January 21 Tracy and I attended a dinner meeting hosted by Mike Beldon and his wife, Louise, at the Fig Tree restaurant on the River Walk. We were joined by Sonny Collins and his friend Penelope Speier; Nick Hollis and his wife, Liecie; and Sculley and her husband, Mike. Collins and Hollis are on the board of directors of the San Antonio River Foundation, created by SARA to raise private funds for the river.

Collins had invited Ed Uhlir to be our guest of honor. Uhlir was director of design, architecture, and landscape for the twenty-three-acre Millennium Park, built on an industrial site in downtown Chicago and completed in 2004. Private and public funds converted the site into a unique combination of cultural venues. The main features are the outdoor Jay Pritzker Pavilion, the Cloud Gate sculpture on AT&T Plaza, Crown Fountain, Lurie Garden, and the Joan W. and Irving B. Harris Theater for Music and Dance. After explaining how the park developed, Uhlir said, "The culture park now defines Chicago to the world. You have that same opportunity with the thirteen-mile River Walk extension."

The next day I met with Peak, now an executive with AT&T, and Whitacre in his office to discuss how best to approach business leaders who were gathering in a conference room down the hall. After a half-hour discussion on how to pitch them for financial support, we went into the room. Uhlir spoke about the development of Millennium Park and its economic impact on Chicago. Then Whitacre announced that AT&T would pledge $5 million to the river project and encouraged other business leaders to donate.

Meanwhile negotiations with Zachry dragged on for five weeks. At the end of Feburary Hardberger, Sculley, City Attorney Michael Bernard, County Attorney Ed Schweninger, Seth Mitchell, my chief of staff, and Joe Aceves, executive director of infrastructure services for the county, met in my office to review the status. Hardberger suggested that the landscaping and bridge be dropped from the bid, saving $4.6 million. On the base bid and sidewalk, Zachry would do the work for $49.8 million, still some $6 million above our highest cost estimate. Hardberger suggested that he and I meet with David Zachry, president and COO of the company.

At our meeting Zachry said he might be able to do some value engineering, but it would have little effect on his price. I said I could not recommend the contract unless he would let an independent estimator hired by the city or county review his bid documents and tell us whether the cost was appropriate. He agreed, and the city contracted with PBS&J to review the bid.

In the meantime SARA found a way to bail both the county and city out of their financial jam. Under the tri-party contract, the city was responsible for river maintenance. SARA would take over its maintenance, which would save the city $1.5 million annually. The city could use the money to amortize the debt on the project's cost overrun.

Over the weekend of March 24 Tracy and I met Hardberger and businessman Eugene Simor in Port Aransas for a day of boating. Hardberger and Simor had been sailing together for more than ten years. We boarded Hardberger's stunning two-story, forty-two-foot boat, which had been built to his specifications and featured a beautiful teakwood finish. As we traveled the intracoastal canal, Hardberger showed me a letter from John German, vice president of PBS&J, stating that "Zachry has prepared a best and final offer that is fair and reasonable."

"This satisfies me," I said. "Let's move forward."

We went to Charles Butt's lighthouse at Port Aransas, just off the intracoastal canal in the middle of a marsh with no road access. Phil and Linda's colorful friends Rick Reichenbach and Regina Payton manage the property, living in one of three historic buildings next to the lighthouse. The day was so relaxing I could see why it was hard for Hardberger to give up sailing to become San Antonio's mayor.

The next Monday I saw Sculley in Washington, D.C., on the annual S.A. to D.C. trip, hosted by the Greater San Antonio and Hispanic Chambers of Commerce. At a reception at the Organization of American States, she told me the agreement with SARA was progressing well and would cover both our cost over-runs. I said, "Your and Phil's tough dealing with SARA helped get them to incur this additional cost." She smiled and said nothing.

On April 3 Hardberger, Sculley, Rowe, Rothe, Collins, and I met to complete the understanding among the three parties. Sculley agreed to take the proposal to city council, recommending an issuance of $18 million in debt. The annual $1.5 million the city would save by SARA's maintaining the uban section of the Museum Reach would cover the debt. Hardberger concluded, "This is the most important thing anyone in this room will do in his or her life. We need to stay together as a unit." On April 10 Commissioners Court approved the contract, followed by SARA on April 11 and city council on April 12. But more than two months of hard work preceded those three days of quick action.

Should we have rebid the project? We will know the answer within two years, when the project should be completed. I bet we took the right action.

On a pleasant blue-sky morning on May 8, we had the ceremonial beginning of the big dig with a large Zachry backhoe. To honor the Indians who first settled on the San Antonio River, Linda Ximenes sprinkled the headwaters to the east, west, south, and north, to heavens above and mother earth below, in a traditional blessing of the native Tap Pilam Coahuiltecan Nation. This day would not have occurred in a timely fashion without Hardberger's aggressive and strong leadership.

With the northern Museum Reach under construction, residents of the South Side began to express dissatisfaction over the fact that work had not begun on the Mission Reach. The project was under the control of the Army Corps of Engineers, but they did not have the funding to begin construction. In order to jump-start it, Commissioners Court passed an order on July 24 agreeing to advance fund $21.6 million to get the first phase under construction.

In early October Congress passed a bill allowing the advance funding and providing a payback to the county if federal funding is approved in the future. On October 12 we held a groundbreaking ceremony on the river in Concepción Park. I stated that I felt the nine-mile Mission Reach was the most important part of the project because of the environmental restoration of the river. Over 24,000 native trees and fifty-six acres of native grass would be planted; 113 acres of aquatic habitat and 320 acres of riverside habitat would be restored. I pointed out that four of the five court members—Elizondo, Rodriguez, Adkisson, and me—grew up on the South Side close to the river. I said we were committed to providing the funding to complete the project.

As this book goes to press we continue to seek federal funding for the Mission Reach. The Commissioners Court is also working on additional local funding for both the Mission Reach and the park segment of the Museum Reach from Josephine Street north to Hildebrand Avenue, stretching through Brackenridge Park. This section will include ecosystem restoration, removal of concrete drainage, and enhancement of four bridge crossings.

In addition to the funding Commissioners Court provided from the flood control tax, we took the first step toward using the hotel-motel tax as an additional source. On May 22, 2007, we approved the appointment of a San Antonio River task force to recommend up to $75 million in river improvement projects. The funding would be subject to approval by the court and submitted to the voters as part of the extension of the hotel-motel tax. The measure is scheduled to go before the voters in May 2008. The Commissioners Court is committed to completing what could be the most important public works project in San Antonio of our time.

FIVE

· · · · · · · · · · · · · · · · · ·

The Impact

THE AT&T CENTER, the PGA Village, Toyota Motor Corp., and the San Antonio River Walk extension—all have had major impacts on the community in many different ways. And if San Antonio makes the right moves they will continue to do so for many years.

Toyota Motor Corp. has had the greatest significance, changing both our economy and our economic strategy. It has influenced patterns of city growth, acting as a catalyst for South Side development, and has helped bring about changes in our rail system.

The AT&T Center has enhanced the San Antonio Stock Show & Rodeo, and, by keeping the Spurs in the city long term, increased the city's visibility, bringing a positive image to the world stage that could not have been purchased with advertising dollars.

Both the PGA Village and the San Antonio River Walk extension offer a boon to one of the city's major economic generators—tourism. Both will draw more people to the city for longer periods and will improve the quality of life for those who live here. The PGA Village also set a new standard for a planned environmental development. The four-mile Museum Reach of the river will stimulate economic development, and the nine-mile Mission Reach will enhance our environment.

Woven throughout the story of these projects is evidence of the county's growing power and stature, a trend that will become more pronounced with the continued use of public improvement districts to provide services for populations in areas of the county that the city does not annex. The county's expanding role will also be exhibited in its use of the hotel-motel tax, derived from paying off the arena debt early, to address a number of community needs.

ECONOMIC POLICY

"You would be able to split the economic history of San Antonio between 'before Toyota' and 'after Toyota,' " Eugenio Alemán, a senior economist for Wells Fargo, said in the bank's July 2006 report, the *San Antonio Express-News* reported. That is not an exaggeration. San Antonio's economy is booming and becoming more diversified.

Toyota had a major impact on local and state economic policy. Before Toyota, the state played virtually no role in attracting companies to Texas. Before Toyota, the San Antonio Economic Development Foundation, or EDF, often operated at odds with the city and county. We fought over the requirement of a living wage and over the amount and length of tax abatements. The EDF refused to share their prospect list with us. Before Toyota, the city and county had different tax abatement policies.

After Toyota, we used the experience of working together to reorganize our way of doing business. In early 2004 Mayor

Ed Garza and I organized a "big five" economic working group consisting of representatives of the San Antonio Water System, CPS Energy, the city, the county, and the EDF. We agreed to meet monthly.

Joining Garza and me at our first meeting were Jim Mayor, San Antonio Water System chairman, and David Chardavoyne, president; Aurora Ortega-Geis, CPS Energy chairperson, and Milton Lee, president; Ed Kelley, EDF chairman, and Mario Hernandez, president; Ramiro Cavazos and David Marquez, the city and county economic development directors, respectively. We developed a number of operating principles and agreed to share information. The EDF gave us their prospect list for the first time, enabling us to be helpful early on in convincing companies to locate in San Antonio. We developed a unified tax abatement policy that set clear criteria for financial incentives and required companies to pay a living wage. The city and county later adopted a unified policy. We also created a strategy to target manufacturing companies.

At each of our monthly meetings, Hernandez briefed our working group on the status of potential prospects. He told us their requests so each governmental entity could address their needs. To keep the names of prospects secret, we referred to them under code names such as Project Hawk, Project X, Project Doc Holiday, Project Blue Moon, and Project Foxtrot.

After Toyota, we successfully lobbied the 2003 Texas legislature to create a $250 million Texas Enterprise Fund. We established lines of communication with the governor's economic development office to lay the groundwork for an economic grant.

In addition Garza took the lead in convincing the city council to set aside $12 million for a local economic development fund to attract state economic development funds.

To supplement the city fund, we convinced CPS Energy to create an additional fund. In January 2005 the CPS board agreed to convert its $43 million Electrical Overhead Conversion Fund into a Community Infrastructure and Economic Development Fund. One percent of electricity revenue had funded the plan, which was expected to grow by some $10 million a year. The plan called for targeting industries including aerospace/aviation, biotechnology/health services, automotive/advanced manufacturing, financial services, Internet, information technology, and telecommunications that would need a lot of kilowatt energy.

Between the two local economic development funds, we gave grants to attract an expansion of Maxim Integrated Products, $1.5 million; Washington Mutual, $3 million; DPT Laboratories and Brooks City-Base, $1.5 million; seventeen Toyota suppliers, $1.1 million; and a Microsoft Data Center, $5.2 million.

After Toyota, the EDF began running advertisements in trade magazines that read, "Serious automotive money is riding on San Antonio. Be part of the action." It listed the Toyota suppliers who had agreed to come. Usually the EDF's prospect list included 30 percent manufacturing firms. After Toyota's decision and the ads, the list was up to 47.1 percent manufacturing.

The largest manufacturing firm we corralled post-Toyota was Sino Swearingen Aircraft Corp. The process to secure Sino is a good example of how we worked together. In 1987 Ed Swearingen, a successful aviation pioneer, announced that he planned to build a private jet airplane. He began designing the aircraft in a small warehouse along a runway at the seldom-used Stinson Field next to Mission Park Cemetery on San Antonio's South Side.

Businessman Douglas Jaffe invested $9 million in Swearingen's company with a handshake at a Jim's Coffee Shop. Swearingen named his proposed jet SJ 30. SJ stood for Swearingen-Jaffe. Over the years, as he continued his research and development, it became clear that he would need significant long-term investment to carry the plane through testing and production. In 1995 Sen. Jay Rockefeller introduced him to Taiwanese government officials and businessmen, and the Taiwanese government invested more than $600 million over several years. Some of the work took place in San Antonio and in West Virginia. In 2005 Sino Swearingen began the process of deciding at which location to manufacture the plane.

That summer Kelly Simmons, Sino Swearingen's chief financial officer, called to say that airport officials had told him they could not provide the twenty acres of land they needed for manufacturing. I told him to let me see what I could do and then called Sheryl Sculley, who would become city manager on November 1. When I told her about the problem, she said, "I believe the airport land should be used to create good-paying jobs, not to get the highest rent. I'll get to work on it."

"You are a blessing," I told her.

At the end of October Sino Swearingen completed the final FFA test, becoming certified to begin production and to sell the SJ 30, a seven-seat jet that would become the world's fastest and longest-range light business aircraft.

My son Kevin, a city councilman, and I had lunch with Dr. Ching Kuo, chairman and CEO of Sino Swearingen, to assure him of city and county support. Kevin and Commissioner Lyle Larson met with Rep. Joe Straus and Sen. Jeff Wentworth, who agreed to help them with a grant from the state. Hernandez and his board members also worked on the grant. CPS Energy and the San Antonio Water System worked with Sino to set up a favorable rate structure on water and electrical power. Both the city and county granted the promised tax abatements. The city provided a lease for the airport land.

In February 2006 I joined Simmons at Nelson Wolff Municipal Stadium, the home of the San Antonio Missions, on a cold, overcast day to watch his son catch for Army during a ballgame with Kentucky. During the game he told me: "We're pleased with the local effort. If you're able to get the state economic grant, I believe we have a deal." We later secured a $2.5 million state economic grant.

Finally, after one year of working on the project, Gov. Rick Perry, Phil Hardberger, and I hosted a press conference on July 29 in the City Hall media room to announce that San Antonio had captured the manufacturing plant, which would employ 800 workers with an average salary of $50,000.

Although Sino Swearingen began to produce planes, they would have difficulties after the Taiwanese government changed hands and the subsequent administration sold the company to Action Aviation Investors. It remains to be seen how the company will do under new ownership.

After establishing the state economic development fund, we lobbied the 2005 legislature to create a $200 million emerging technology fund to be used for collaborations, investments, research grants, and talent recruitment. The legislation created eight Regional Centers of Innovation and Commercialization. We effectively lobbied Governor Perry to appoint David Spenser chairman of a seventeen-member committee to recommend what projects to fund. Spenser and I had co-chaired the San Antonio Technology Accelerator Initiative, or SATAI, an organization created to build a strong technology base in San Antonio. Under his leadership, the panel named SATAI the Regional Center of Innovation and Commercialization for the San Antonio area. SATAI became the model for the regional centers to imitate. In 2006 Spenser announced $2.85 million in grants to three San Antonio firms—CardioSpectra Inc., Xilas Medical Inc., and Bauhaus Software Inc. Another $4.1 million went to UTSA's information security program.

The most interesting development in our technology industry came about thanks to the innovative thinking of the mayor of a small suburban municipality and the CEO of a home-grown technology company. It set the stage for what could be San Antonio's equivalent of Austin's Dell Corporation.

In 2005 Windcrest Mayor Jack Leonhardt visited with Commissioner Adkisson and me regarding his city's vision to revitalize the Walzem Road area just east of IH-35, where the abandoned sixty-nine acre, 1.2 million square-foot Windsor Park Mall was located. He asked the county to participate in developing a revitalization plan. We contributed funds to the cost and played a role in creating the plan, which identified the mall as an excellent location for a large service company. One potential service company was

Rackspace Managed Housing, founded in 1998 when three Trinity University students—Pat Condon, Dirk Elmendorf, and Richard Yoo—teamed up with local entrepreneur Graham Weston. Since its founding, Rackspace has grown to 1,900 employees—called Rackers—1,300 of whom are in San Antonio. It is the largest and fastest-growing IT hosting specialist, with customers around the world.

In summer 2005 Leonhardt approached Rackspace officials about moving their headquarters to the mall site. While Rackspace liked the idea, nothing could be done until the City of San Antonio agreed to transfer the site to Windcrest city limits and a tax incentive plan could be implemented.

On August 15, 2006, Leonhardt, accompanied by Windcrest City Administrator Ronnie Cain, Ray Watson, executive director of the Windcrest Economic Development Corporation (WEDC), and Walzem Road Area Revitalization President Terry Williams, met with Adkisson, Bexar County Executive Director David Marquez, and me in my office. Leonhardt told us he wanted WEDC to buy the mall site, take it off the tax roles, and lease it to Rackspace. He asked for my help convincing the City of San Antonio to transfer the site. After the meeting I took Leonhardt over to City Hall and introduced him to Mayor Hardberger, who suggested he meet with city staff. He did, but he was initially not well received. The city did not want to give up the taxable mall and surrounding land.

Six months later I met with Leonhardt and an investment group headed up by Gary Cain, Jeremy Hebet, and Michael White. The group would provide funding for the purchase of the mall site as well as an additional 284 acres for future development. I told them I supported their plan.

To nudge the City of San Antonio along, Leonhardt persuaded Reps. Joe Straus and Ruth Jones McClendon and Senator Wentworth to sponsor a bill that allowed the mall site to be transferred into Windcrest. After the bill passed, the city in August 2007 reached a revenue sharing plan with Windcrest in exchange for boundary changes. Windcrest then negotiated a thirty-year lease with Rackspace; the company agreed to spend $100 million in improvements to the mall.

The state gave a $22 million grant to Rackspace provided they create an additional 4,000 jobs within five years. The deal was concluded with Rackspace and all four governmental agencies: the state, the City of San Antonio, the City of Windcrest, and Bexar County.

After the final agreement, I had lunch with Weston, chairman of Rackspace, at Bohanan's Prime Steak and Seafood Restaurant on downtown Houston Street. He said: "We want Rackspace to be part of the fabric of the local community and encourage other tech businesses to relocate to the area. We want to develop Tech Town where the tech community can congregate, share ideas, and create a tech-friendly identity for our city. I don't want our campus to be closed off, unapproachable by our new neighbors. Perhaps a coffee shop, a fitness center, a restaurant, and outdoor music venues can be located on our site to share with our neighbors and the tech community at large."

Leonhardt had accomplished the seemingly impossible. He had the right project and a terrific company in Rackspace. The tax incentive plan was an aggressive and unique proposal. Incentives like this should only be used when they create jobs and revitalize a declining area of the county. Leonhardt taught us all a new lesson in economic development.

Another key development in the technology field was bringing Microsoft to San Antonio. For two years we encouraged Microsoft officials to locate a data center in the city, and thanks to the newly created CPS Energy incentive package we were finally able to. On July 31, 2007, Microsoft broke ground on a 470,000 square-foot building located on forty-four acres in Westover Hills. They will serve up web pages, instant messages, photos, videos, e-mail accounts, and search information for millions of Internet users.

The nation is beginning to take notice of San Antonio's technology sector. *Business 2.0* magazine in its May 2007 issue ranked San Antonio first in the nation, with the highest job-growth rate for college-educated technology and business professionals. We had a growth rate of 8.9 percent in the last year.

After Toyota, we were ready to expand our economic policy by intensifying our international reach. We targeted China; its economy was growing three times faster than the U.S. economy. Millions of hybrid businesses mixed their financial interest with local governmental bodies. More than 30 million private entrepreneurial businesses made up one-third of China's GDP; foreign investment made up another third. If China's growth continued at that pace, it soon would become the largest economy in the world. It was time for us to develop a relationship with China as we had nurtured with Japan prior to landing Toyota.

At noon on August 3, 2005, Mayor Hardberger and I, along with our delegation, landed at Pudong International Airport outside the historic city of Shanghai, near the confluence of the Huangpu and Yangtze rivers on the East China Sea. Founded in the eleventh century as a fishing village, Shanghai is now home to some 15 million people and one of the world's five greatest commercial centers.

As we drove into the city we passed thousands of multistory, unair-conditioned tenements. Near the city center the landscape changed into thousands of high-rise skyscrapers that would dwarf the New York skyline. At the downtown Ritz Carlton, hotel officials and pretty young women with arms full of flowers greeted us. A thriving shopping district surrounded the state-of-the-art hotel, which had every possible amenity.

The next morning we met with representatives of twelve logistic companies. Bruce Miller, president of San Antonio's Port Authority, formerly KellyUSA; David Marquez, Bexar County director of economic development; and Blake Hastings, president of the Free Trade Alliance, made the case that the Mexican ports of Lázaro Cárdenas and Mazatlán were viable alternatives to expensive California ports. A shipper using the Mexican ports would send goods to the United States on rail lines running through Laredo to San Antonio, where they could be distributed, along with value-added manufacturing.

The next day we met with Shanghai's Vice Mayor Zhou Yu Peng, a powerful player in local economic development projects. The last two chairmen of the Communist Party had been mayors of Shanghai. After a discussion on investment opportunities in San Antonio, he invited us back to the World Fair Expo, which will take place in Shanghai in 2010.

That afternoon we visited the business sector of Pudong across the Huangpu River from Shanghai. Fifteen years earlier it had been a swampy rural area. Today Pudong is home to thousands of foreign companies, including three hundred Fortune 500 companies. That night we had dinner with Chinese officials at the Peace Hotel on the Bund, a boulevard along the Huangpu River that links parks and European-style buildings constructed in the late nineteenth and early twentieth century.

We then traveled to Beijing and met Elisa Chan, president of the Alamo Asian American Chamber of Commerce. Chan had traveled earlier to Beijing, where she has an apartment. That night Chinese businessman Yu Yongquian hosted us at the famous Beijing Roast Duck Restaurant. I never knew a duck had so many parts. I believe we ate all of them.

The next day Yu took us to the Shunyi District, where his business is located next to the international airport. We toured the logistic center and visited the Hyundai automobile manufacturing company. Then we lunched with district head Li Ping and several of his colleagues. Li Ping, who must approve all foreign contracts and economic projects in the district, was clearly the key to success for any Chinese businessman or foreign investor doing business there. Numerous other economic districts are located throughout China. Over lunch we were obliged to have numerous toasts with a strong malt drink. By the end of the meal we were feeling no pain and had become the best of friends. We learned that if we were to be successful, we needed to have strong contacts with local government officials and Chinese businessmen. A little drink helps.

Returning home the next day, we thought we had made a good first step into China. We met high governmental officials and established good business ties. We visited two of the country's three major economic centers. The third economic center lies in southern China in Guangzhou province, adjacent to Hong Kong. And, although Hardberger and I did not visit Guangzhou, part of our delegation did. Miller, Marquez, and Hastings met with several Guangzhou businessmen and government officials. A few weeks later I hosted a dinner at Mi Tierra Restaurant back home for a delegation from Guangzhou.

We took a step toward linking San Antonio to the Mexican ports of Mazatlán and Lázaro Cárdenas by signing a trade agreement with their port authorities designating Port San Antonio a port of entry from Mexico. An alliance of the city, county, San Antonio Port Authority, and Free Trade Alliance hired the husband-and-wife team of Sun Hui and Harley Seyedin to represent us in Shanghai and the Guangzhou province. We hope they will be as successful as Naoko Shirane and her late husband have been with Japan. The process has begun.

We will continue to work on the new economic policies we adopted after attracting Toyota. Since then the city has attracted eighty companies, including thirty-five manufacturing firms. Thousands of jobs have been created; in fact, 2005 and 2006 are the best two years we have had in job creation. In April 2007 our unemployment rate fell to 3.6 percent.

TOURISM

The county's arena lease provided the Spurs with the financial strength to build a sustainable, winning franchise. According to *Forbes Magazine*, the Spurs franchise's value increased from $122 million in 1998 when the team played in the Alamodome to $334 million in 2004 after it moved to the arena. In 2004 the Spurs ranked eighth among the twenty-nine NBA franchises in value, and the arena deal was the main reason for the value's increase.

Investors in other cities were in hot pursuit of the Spurs before the arena was built. The team could have gone the way of the Vancouver Grizzlies, which moved to Memphis in 2001, or the Charlotte Hornets, which moved to New Orleans in 2002. The Maloof brothers, who made a play for the Spurs, could have taken them to their hometown of Albuquerque. By building the arena and committing the Spurs to a twenty-five-year lease, Bexar County ensured that the franchise will stay in San Antonio. In what is thought to be the strongest NBA nonrelocation agreement, the Spurs would be required to pay a yearly declining $300 million penalty if the team moved. The team is tied to San Antonio for the long term, and that's good for marketing the city and attracting tourists.

The Spurs have won three full-season championships since they moved into the arena in 2003. Although the championships have not been back to back, four in the last nine years have many sports writers calling the team a dynasty. Financial stability has allowed the team to assemble a strong basketball staff led by Gregg Popovich, executive vice president of basketball operations and head coach. Popovich has won four rings, establishing himself as one of the greatest coaches in NBA history. R. C. Buford, senior vice president and general manager, and the rest of the coaches and staff have also played critical roles during the championship years. The Spurs have been able to establish a strong management staff headed by Rick Pych, executive vice president of finance and corporate development, and Russ Bookbinder, executive vice president of business operations.

The city's visibility has increased dramatically because of the inclusion of five international players. Tony Parker of France, Manu Ginobili and Fabricio Oberto of Argentina, Tim Duncan of the U.S. Virgin Islands, and Francisco Elson of The Netherlands have attracted television audiences around the world. In addition, David Robinson and Tim Duncan have played on the U.S. Olympic basketball team. The 2007 NBA finals between the Spurs and the Cleveland Cavaliers were broadcast live to 205 countries in forty-six languages. This record made the NBA the most international of U.S. major league sports.

While it is impossible to place a monetary value on a city's international profile, the Spurs are clearly critical to projecting a positive image of San Antonio. During a 2007 NBA finals game, *Express-News* columnist Ken Rodriguez clocked five and a half minutes of international television exposure for the Alamo, the River Walk, and other San Antonio landmarks. A Nielsen survey showed that more than 9 million U.S. viewers tuned in to the game. With that audience, Rodriguez calculated the advertising time to cost $4.5 million. The convention center advertising budget for the year is only $3.2 million.

Spurs Sports & Entertainment has attracted more than 4 million guests to some 450 events in the AT&T Center in its first four years of operation. The San Antonio Rampage ice hockey team, a top minor league affiliate of the Phoenix Coyotes, and the WNBA San Antonio Silver Stars are owned by the Spurs and play there.

When the Spurs left the Alamodome for the AT&T Center, the loss caused a financial hardship for the dome. But it also offered the city an opportunity to use the dome to attract more convention-related business. City Manager Sculley combined the Alamodome and convention center operations into one entity, and in April 2007 she convinced the city council to appropriate $8.3 million in upgrades to the dome. And although the dome does not make money booking convention business, the bookings provide an economic boost for the city. According to a 2004 study commissioned by the San Antonio Area Tourism Council, the local hospitality industry is an $8.7 billion business—and growing. Approximately 21 million visitors came to the city in 2004. In 2005 room nights were up 8.5 percent over 2004, ranking San Antonio third in the top twenty-five markets nationally; the following year revenue moved the city to the top position.

The increase in tourism has led to a hotel boom. In March 2007 Bruce Ford, senior vice president of New Hampshire–based Lodging Econometrics, announced that more hotels were being built in San Antonio than in any other U.S. city, with forty-four hotels and 7,360 hotel rooms under construction or expected to break ground within a year. The 1,000-room Grand Hyatt San Antonio, a convention center hotel, is scheduled for completion in 2008. It will be the second tallest building downtown, second only to the Tower of the Americas. Hyatt officials say advanced bookings have far exceeded their projections. The Alamodome's convention business will increase as new downtown hotels open their doors.

While the Spurs and the AT&T Center have impacted tourism, the PGA Village's impact will be much more dramatic. The development will be home to the city's first Tournament Players Club golf courses. The first TPC course, built in 1981 at Sawgrass in Ponte Vedra Beach, Florida, became the prototype for several other TPC courses built around the nation. Large enough to create a natural amphitheater with spectator areas, these courses are home to major PGA Tour events and an attraction for business golfers. The PGA Village courses, designed by Pete Dye and Greg Norman, will become a model for the next generation of TPC courses.

Golf San Antonio stages the Texas Open at La Cantera in northwest San Antonio. In early 2007 Golf San Antonio CEO Tony Piazzi told me:

> The Texas Open is played at the La Cantera golf course, which is not a TPC course. With a non-TPC course and a small hotel, we're not able to secure a favorable time on the PGA Tour schedule. Hence we don't attract the best golf professionals. Moving the Texas Open from La Cantera to the two new TPC courses will be as important to the Texas Open as the new arena was to the Spurs. I believe the PGA Tour will reschedule the Texas Open in the spring, which will help us attract the top-rated golfers and a highly rated television broadcast.

The adjoining 1,002-room JW Marriott San Antonio Hill Country Resort and Spa will have more than 140,000 square feet of customized indoor space that will include 21,000 square-foot and 40,000 square-foot banquet halls, 40,000 square feet of exhibit halls, and nineteen meeting breakout rooms. It also will include a 26,000 square-foot, world-class spa. The hotel will have room to host a large golf trade show concurrent with the Texas Open and will also attract other conventions and business conferences. Their delegates will be eager to play on the two state-of-the-art golf courses. When CEOs of major corporations visit the PGA Village for the PGA tournament or a convention, they will get a taste of San Antonio. The PGA Village will bring more people to the city who make decisions about where to locate or move a branch, division, or perhaps an entire company.

The PGA Village also will give San Antonio the opportunity to evolve into a major golf destination similar to the Phoenix area. The JW Marriott resort hotel will join the Westin La Cantera and Hyatt Hill Country Resort to give us three major golf and resort destinations. Just one month after the Marriott groundbreaking, Gaylord Entertainment & Co. met with Hardberger and me to say they would buy the Westin La Cantera, with plans to double the number of rooms and add 160,000 square feet of meeting space. With our year-round pleasant weather, our golf resort industry should continue to grow. More than 28 million people play golf in the United States, and half of them play eight or more times a year. Many of them are waiting to come to San Antonio.

The thirteen-mile San Antonio River Walk extension also will play a role in attracting tourists. A study by economist Jon

Hockenyos of public policy consulting firm TXP cited a finding that 77 percent of North American travelers have been on a trip involving nature and outdoor adventure. Their top-ranked activities were casual walking, wildlife viewing, and hiking. Another study by John Kaatz of Conventions, Sports & Leisure International found that the river experience is the single most important aspect of San Antonio's visitor industry.

The nine-mile Mission Reach, which extends south to Mission Espada, will offer tourists an opportunity for outdoor activity in a unique setting. The hike-and-bike trails beside the river will allow them to see the newly established 113 acres of aquatic habitat and 320 acres of riverside habitat with thousands of native trees. They can connect to the Mission Trail Parkway and take hike-and-bike trails through Mission Espada Park. They also can enjoy Mission County Park or Concepción Park on the riverbanks. During their hike, they can visit the four historic missions. An amphitheater at the confluence of San Pedro Creek and the San Antonio River will offer outdoor live music and theatrical performances.

CITY SOUTH

A personal glimpse of the South Side offers a sense of how far it fell behind the rest of the city's development and how important Toyota's impact will be for its emergence.

My grandparents, Adolph and Emma Wolff, along with my dad and his sister and brother, moved from Pflugerville, Texas, to San Antonio in the early 1930s and settled on the South Side among several German American families. My dad went to Page Junior High School and, had he not dropped out in 1936, would have gone to Brackenridge High School. Instead he went to work for the Majestic Oil Company on South Flores. He picked the right place, because he had lunch at the Red Top Inn down the street from the company. My mother, Marie, who had also quit school, worked as a waitress there for her cousins, Billie Jo and Myrtle Williams. My mom was a looker, and Dad fell for her pretty quickly.

My parents' decision to drop out of school mirrored that of the vast majority of young, working-class men and women during the Depression. They had to work to support their families. By 1939, the year my parents married, Mom was scooping ice cream for Better Home Ice Cream and Dad was stacking lumber for Campbell Lumber Company. They moved into a small home on McKinley Avenue just off Presa Street. My paternal grandparents lived with them. My grandfather worked as a janitor at the McKinley Avenue Baptist Church on the corner of Presa and McKinley, and my grandmother took care of the house, earning a little money taking in laundry.

I was born in my parents' bedroom at 9 A.M. on October 27, 1940. Dr O. S. Moore and my grandmother assisted in the birth as Grandpa and Dad watched. Dr. Moore charged my dad $15. Less than two years later my brother George was born at home on Regina Street. By 1947, when my brother Gary was born, my parents had enough money for Mom to give birth at Baptist Hospital.

Populated by working middle-class families, our side of town was a special place to grow up. We were free to play anywhere because neighbors knew each other, streets were safe, and no one locked their doors. We swam at Hot Wells and had family picnics at Roosevelt Park. We went to nine-cent Saturday matinees and traded comics we bought at the local grocery. We walked to school. I went to Laura Steele Elementary, then Riverside Elementary, and then Page Junior High School. Baseball was our game. We played sandlot baseball on Saturdays at Kite Field on Fair Avenue. George and I also played for the McCreless Homebuilders in the Laura Steele Little League. We were batboys for the Texas Consolidated Transporters, a semipro team that played at Richter Field across from Mission Stadium. As members of the knothole gang, we cheered for the Missions in the Texas AA League.

My only bad childhood memory is of the wind blowing the wrong way. When that happened we could smell the horrible odor of everyone's waste, which had been deposited in Mitchell Lake south of our home after being processed at the Rilling Road Wastewater Treatment Plant a short distance upstream. Because San Antonio slopes south, it was easy for the city to send all that waste our way.

When I was thirteen, in 1953, my father was transferred to Houston; we lived there until after I graduated from Bellaire High School in 1959. When we came back to San Antonio, the South Side had begun a downward spiral, and we chose to live on the North Side.

The city grew north because the South Side got all the bad stuff and the North Side got all the goodies. The international airport, the medical center, and the best schools went to the North Side. Landfills, sewer plants, and dirty coal-generating electrical power plants landed on the South Side. Two freeway systems, IH-37 and IH-35, built in the 1950s and 1960s, ripped the heart out of South Side neighborhoods. The house where I was born, on McKinley, was a victim of the IH-37 freeway. The Army Corps of Engineers added to the insult when it made a drainage ditch out of the San Antonio River. On top of all this dirty laundry, rainwater from the North Side flooded South Side streets. As the downward spiral continued, most South Siders who came into a few dollars moved north to where the better homes and jobs were.

During my terms on the city council and then as mayor, we took steps to help the South Side. In 1987, my first year as a council member, we closed the Rilling Road Wastewater Treatment Plant that sent waste to Mitchell Lake. We created the Mitchell Lake wetlands out of what had been a sewage lagoon. We flooded more than 200 of the 589 acres with treated wastewater to provide a year-round refuge for more than 314 species of migratory birds, making it one of the largest bird refuges in the United States. We bought additional land around Mitchell Lake, bringing the total to more than 1,300 acres, and improved the roadway and built an educational center. Today the National Audubon Society manages the Mitchell Lake wildlife refuge and wetlands, which has become a major tourist attraction for those interested in viewing the thousands of migratory birds that stop over at the lake.

The city used lake water to irrigate the Mission Del Lago Municipal Golf Course, which was built in 1989 on an adjoining 187 acres. A subdivision of some 200 homes and 200 apartments was later built adjacent to the golf course. The city installed pollution-cleaning devices on the coal-generating electrical plants, implemented several South Side drainage projects, and closed some of the landfills.

The council approved $6.4 million to leverage $25 million in state funding for the Mission Trails project, which included trails from the Alamo ten miles south to connect the other four missions. One route along existing roadways included landscaping, bus shelters, street lamps, and buried electrical lines. Another route along the river included hike-and-bike trails, greenways, and picnic areas.

The city built the San Antonio Police Academy, and the Alamo Community College District built Palo Alto College near Loop 410 South. We also began initial steps toward converting Brooks Air Force Base into Brooks City-Base, a public-private development.

As a South Side boy, I had helped incrementally to revive that part of town, but it was Mayor Garza, a North Side boy and Jefferson High School graduate, who brought a bold new vision to the area. He was a planner by profession, and when he saw the open land to the south he recognized an opportunity to build a community of the future. After being elected mayor in 2001, he presented a plan to city council that focused on some sixty-four square miles of mostly agricultural land south of Loop 410, stretching to Loop 1604 and bounded on the west by IH-35 and on the east by IH-37. The Medina River ran along the area's southern edge.

Some 7,600 people lived in the area. Their per capita income averaged about $10,000, compared to $18,000 for all of Bexar County, and more than 80 percent were Hispanic. Agriculture use accounted for about 30,000 acres of land, with the average farm 80 acres in size. About the only economic development in the area was a stock car racing track and a large flea market.

Garza laid out a conceptual plan to protect large swatches of agricultural land that would surround "new urban" developments made up of mixed housing, retail, commercial, and schools. He envisioned a community where people could walk and ride bikes to work and play. He made the South Side plan his top priority. Most people applauded his vision but thought it was a bit of a pie-in-the-sky dream. They wondered how a plan alone could encourage people to settle in an area that very few had chosen in the last fifty years.

But skepticism did not deter Garza. Like Don Quixote, he drew his sword, saddled up his own Rocinante, and rode south. I assumed the role of Sancho Panza, riding beside him and praising his efforts. We brought along the city's planning director, Emil Moncivais, who sketched out elaborate plans that pleased the mayor.

In order to execute his plan, Garza proposed a limited annexation that gave the city power to zone but not to tax and, therefore, no obligation to provide services. The limited annexation would last for three years, and then the city had to annex fully or let the land remain in the county. The city adopted zoning for and then enacted a limited annexation of fifty-six square miles. Garza also proposed that the Texas legislature pass a bill allowing the city and county to create a Defense Adjustment Management Authority, or DAMA. This special district had the powers to zone and control growth. If the city did not fully annex all the land after the three-year period, the DAMA could be implemented.

All of Garza's planning might have remained on a shelf had Toyota not decided to locate in the middle of his master planned community. This was the first major private investment on the South Side in decades. After Toyota's announcement, investors rushed to purchase land for future development. All of a sudden, people began to think that Garza was one smart cat.

A graduate of Texas A&M University, Garza then sought to capitalize on the Toyota investment by pushing Sen. Frank Madla's dream to build a Texas A&M campus on the South Side. The university was providing upper-level courses on the 126-acre Palo Alto College campus. In February 2003, just seven days after the Toyota announcement, Garza hosted a meeting at the Plaza Club to discuss a strategy to locate an A&M campus on the South Side. Lowry Mays, chairman of the Texas A&M Board of Regents, and former board members Henry Cisneros and Raul Fernandez attended. Acting Chancellor Howard Graves; Leo Sayavedra, vice chancellor for academic and student affairs; businessmen Bartell Zachry and Bill Worth; and I rounded out the group. While some concerns were voiced about the effect the campus would have on the University of Texas at San Antonio, everyone agreed to pursue it.

With the flag of Toyota flying high and the potential for a Texas A&M campus, Garza moved forward with his master plan. In June he released the Southside Initiative Community Plan, a comprehensive document delineating the areas for zoning, parks and open space, transportation arteries, and planned annexation. In October and November the city held hearings on annexation of the first of the proposed zones, 9,796 acres that included the

Toyota site. Naturally, it was targeted first because it was the only zone producing any tax revenue for the city.

Garza and I met with Al Aguilar, CEO of Creative Civilization, to develop a plan to market the South Side. We chose to use the name City South and a logo with an S-shaped river flowing between San Antonio and the Missions. Aguilar went to work developing marketing materials. In mid-October Garza held a press conference at Mission Del Lago Municipal Golf Course to launch the City South initiative. Hundreds of people showed up as he unveiled a flag, caps, and other materials with the City South logo.

By now, private-sector investments were beginning to flow south. HollyHills Development, owned by Dan and Marlene Bailey, had bought some 500 acres across the road from Toyota to build a retail center and a warehouse distribution center. They also gave 142 acres to the city for Medina River Park, which now included 364 acres stretching two and a half miles along the Medina River.

Developers have plotted some 8,000 lots for homes since the Toyota announcement. Houston developer Charlie Turner announced the planned community of Espada. Schaefer Homes and Classic Century Homes started two gated communities. The county created a public improvement district to accommodate building the Preserve at Medina River, a 535-acre, mixed-use development on Watson Road at the intersection of SH 16. In mid-June 2005 Commissioner Chico Rodriguez and I joined Fermin Rajunov of Presto Capital on a trek across acres of large trees and water gushing from an underground spring that created a small lake close to the river.

Meanwhile Garza moved fast to secure a location for Texas

A&M before he was term limited out of office. In January 2005, some five months before his term expired, the city council approved $13 million to buy 400 acres on the corner of Loop 410 and U.S. 281 to give to Texas A&M for its campus. The council approved another $18 million for infrastructure improvements. The campus was still a long way off because Texas A&M did not have state funding to build it. Madla had made several failed attempts to pass a tuition-based funding bill. Time ran out on Garza when his term expired in May.

Mayor Hardberger picked up where Garza had left off. In November the city completed annexation of the 9,796 acres that included the Toyota site but took no action on the remaining five zones because they produced little tax revenue. The next month Hardberger and I appointed members to the DAMA board and named Garza chairman. The board had jurisdiction over the five zones that were not annexed.

In May 2006, during a special legislative session, Madla successfully included $40 million for the campus in a tuition bond bill. Although the bill passed, the legislature still needed to fund it. Hardberger did not want to purchase land until a Texas A&M campus received funding and its board was committed to a site. Several landowners stepped forward with proposals to donate land for the campus. Former county budget manager Marcus Jahns, representing Tom Lozzi and Ralph Lampman, partners in Triple L Management, met with me in October and said they were willing to give 550 acres, located between the Toyota plant and Loop 410, to Texas A&M.

On November 29, the day before the Texas A&M board

planned to consider choosing a site, Houston developer Turner came by to say he would give Texas A&M 400 acres to the east of U.S. 281 along the San Antonio River. This land was adjacent to his Espada planned community. The next day the Texas A&M board heard presentations for two proposals. It also considered the original site Garza had picked and a site south of Loop 1604. After the presentations, the board asked staff to analyze the sites and bring a recommendation to the next meeting in February 2007.

In January I saw Sen. Carlos Uresti at a senate dinner in Austin the night before the legislative session started. He had defeated Madla, who later died in a tragic fire, in the previous election. "A&M asked for $10 million to increase the number of students in their upper-level classes at the Palo Alto campus," he said. "They have to get the student load up from 500 to 1,500 in order to receive the tuition money to build the campus."

After I gave a speech in early February to the San Antonio Mobility Coalition conference at the Crossroads Convention Center, Lampman from Triple L Management told me the Texas A&M board had voted to select their site. "Congratulations," I said. "The city should be dancing in the streets. They won't have to purchase any land." In the 2007 legislative session Uresti secured the $10 million funding for upper-level classes at Palo Alto College. In mid-November I joined Texas A&M University System chancellor Michael McKinney and several members of our legislative delegation at a site dedication ceremony.

Toyota also had an impact on commercial activity along Southwest Military Drive. The South Chamber, under the leadership of President Cindy Taylor, took the lead in promoting economic development along the road. My friend John Feik, president and COO of DFB Pharmaceuticals, the parent company of DPT Laboratories, built a 254,000 square-foot building at Brooks City-Base and employed 175 technicians. Trip Pilgrim, president and CEO of the Baptist Health System, reached an agreement with Brooks City-Base to build a major medical building and hospital. Mark Granados built a major retail development adjacent to Brooks City-Base. South Park Mall, which had been languishing, began to thrive with new tenants and shoppers.

Toyota's decision to locate on the South Side has laid the foundation for the area's continuing economic growth. The South Side is coming alive after a fifty-year decline.

EAST SIDE

Interstate 37, built during the 1960s, became a physical and psychological barrier that isolated the East Side from downtown. While investments and economic development flourished downtown, it stopped at IH-37 and the East Side slipped into economic stagnation.

In 1988 Mayor Henry Cisneros revived hopes for the area when he proposed building the $200 million Alamodome just east of IH-37, sandwiched between the railroad tracks and the highway, north of Durango Street and south of East Commerce Street. His decision received overwhelming support from the African American community, which had settled the East Side and comprised the majority of the population. The dome opened in 1993, becoming home to the Spurs and hosting many other major sports and entertainment events. Although it was a huge success, the surrounding area did not take off. According to city statistics, the area within one mile of the dome declined by 2,200 residents, or 13 percent, from 1990 to 2000.

Finally, five years after the Alamodome opened, new development did occur. Bartell Zachry leased the historic Sunset Station, located next to the Alamodome's north parking lot. He spent millions restoring the depot and converting it into an entertainment center. He contracted with Graham Central Station to manage and provide performances and leased part of the facility to Aldaco's Mexican Cuisine.

In April 2007 Zachry told me:

> We were never successful at Sunset Station. When the Spurs moved to the AT&T Center in 2003, what business we did have was really hurt. Graham Central Station failed, and our company had to take over operations of Sunset Station and simply lease the space out for special events. In addition to Sunset Station, I bought some of the buildings in St. Paul Square [across the street from Sunset Station]. In 2000 I located Ruth's Chris Steak House in one of the buildings, and it got off to a very slow start. I purchased the St. Paul church and turned it into a special event venue. I was pouring money down a continuous black hole, but I didn't want to give up so I kept investing.

The situation was no better around the AT&T Center, which opened ten years after the Alamodome began operations. Spurs fans enjoyed traveling on the upgraded streets, but as soon as the game was over they jumped in their cars and went home. No new economic activity occurred around the arena.

Two East Side economic studies were commissioned. In April 2003 Economics Research Associates released a study noting that the city-owned Willow Springs Golf Course, across the street from the AT&T Center, offered an opportunity for economic development. In 2004 the Urban Land Institute reported that the IH-37 underpasses linking downtown to the East Side needed to be more inviting. It also found that hotel and residential development offered the best opportunity in the Alamodome area. The county, city, and state contracted with artist Bill FitzGibbons to create *Light Channels*, a computer-controlled display of colored lights and digital effects that eliminated the dark, foreboding passage of the underpasses on Houston and Commerce streets. The project was completed in 2006.

While that project was under way, Zachry began work on a hotel and residential development, and in fall 2005 he asked me to encourage VIA President John Milam to sell him some land next to Sunset Station as a site for a hotel. I made the call to Milam, emphasizing how important the hotel project was to the East Side. VIA sold the land to Zachry, and in 2006 construction began on the 109-room Staybridge Suites.

Zachry's next major investment was historic for the East Side. His son-in-law, Jeff Rochelle, envisioned a high-rise condominium across from VIA's Ellis Alley Park & Ride, a couple of blocks north of St. Paul Square, which offered trolley transportation to downtown. Zachry convinced Drake Leddy, a successful developer, to partner with Rochelle to build Vidorra, a luxury high-rise condominium. Leddy told me: "Land on the east side of IH-37 is considerably less expensive than downtown. We purchased the land from VIA at a reasonable price. The lower cost allows us to build a project that is affordable."

In March 2007 Angela Rinehart of the project's sales office told me the condos were 50 percent leased and that she was having great success marketing them to personnel working at Fort Sam Houston, located on the East Side just north of IH-35. Vidorra's success with Fort Sam Houston personnel was destined to become even better. In August 2005 the Base Realignment and Closure Commission approved the consolidation of all medical training at Fort Sam Houston. Several thousand more people will be working there. In 2007 Commissioners Court approved a grant and the city provided a tax abatement for the 154-unit, twenty-story condominium project. Vidorra is currently under construction.

While Zachry was developing projects near the Alamodome, entrepreneur Bill Tidwell began to make things happen around the AT&T Center. Tidwell, who owns the 2,000-employee Cardell Cabinetry on the East Side, purchased the eighty-five-acre Red Berry estate adjacent to the Willow Springs Golf Course in 2003. The estate is named for its former owner, Red Berry, a colorful and notorious gambler. In the 1940s he built a three-story, 12,000 square-foot mansion on his estate and turned it into a gambling casino. In front of the mansion he built a twelve-acre lake. My dad frequented the casino during the 1950s, and I vaguely remember going with my mother and uncle to pick him up in front of the gate that opened onto Gembler Road.

Tidwell turned the estate into a resort for corporate meetings, weddings, and other events. But he had a larger vision. He began working on a plan to combine the Willow Springs course and the Red Berry estate into a resort hotel and conference center, along with residential units. Meanwhile the county developed a plan to expand the buildings on the coliseum site. The upgrade would include renovating the coliseum, improving the AT&T Center, building an equestrian center, and putting in a new street along the east side of the site from Houston Street to IH-37.

In the three-mile area between the Alamodome and the AT&T Center, the board of the East Side Inner City Tax Increment Re-investment Zone Number 11 took steps to assist with economic development. I served on the board, chaired by Councilwoman Sheila McNeil. We provided a grant to the Staybridge Suites, assembled land on Commerce Street for future development, provided a grant to the East Side cemeteries that were proving to be a tourist attraction, and helped fund an East Side sports complex.

Three economy hotels—Best Western Sunset Suites, the Red Roof Inn, and Holiday Inn Express Hotel & Suites—were built near the Alamodome. Former Spurs star David Robinson founded the Carver Academy, a faith-based school on East Commerce next to the historic Carver Community Cultural Center, the focal point of East Side cultural life.

While the city has a long way to go to take advantage of the investment in the two stadiums, we are finally on the road to success.

NORTH DOWNTOWN

Economist Jon Hockenyos's 2007 economic study found that the four-mile Museum Reach, between Lexington Avenue and

Josephine Street, would become an ideal location for multifamily residential development, along with restaurants and shops. He predicted that this section of the River Walk extension would create an output of almost $1 billion and hundreds of millions in earnings annually. Almost 10,000 permanent jobs could be created when the projects are finished. His study also found that the total tax impact to the city should exceed $12.5 million annually.

In order to further capitalize on the Museum Reach's economic boost, other infrastructure improvements were necessary along Broadway, which runs roughly parallel to the San Antonio River. This section of Broadway, between downtown and Josephine Street, deteriorated over the years and lost its economic vitality. Abandoned buildings and deserted car dealerships left a mostly barren asphalt parking lot along large sections of the road.

To further stimulate economic development, in December 2006 the city created a twenty-five-year tax increment district encompassing some fifty-six blocks, primarily along Broadway. The city's economic development department found that using the district's funds to improve infrastructure would lead to 6,000 housing units, 150 hotel rooms, 700,000 square feet of office buildings, and 250,000 square feet of retail. The population would grow from 700 to 9,000 people within twenty years, and property values would increase from $125 million to $1.2 billion.

As mentioned earlier, businessman Kit Goldsbury began developing the Pearl Brewery site even before construction on the river began. George Geis began building retail, apartments, and offices on the four-and-a-half-acre old Smith Chevrolet site two blocks from the Pearl Brewery. James Lifshutz subsequently bought the project and began work to complete it. He also bought and renovated El Tropicano Hotel on the river next to Lexington Avenue. Many more projects will follow.

THE SAN ANTONIO STOCK SHOW & RODEO

The AT&T Center took the San Antonio Livestock Exposition, or SALE, to new heights. The arena increased rodeo seating capacity by 70 percent over the coliseum. In 2003, the rodeo's first year in the center, 1,066,778 fans attended, generating $18.4 million in revenue. Two years later attendance reached 1,095,939, with revenue of $22 million.

Jackie Van De Walle-Dreher described the San Antonio Stock Show & Rodeo as "truly more than cattle, cotton candy, carnival, cowboys, and concerts—the biggest asset is the educational commitment to youth." Increased attendance allowed SALE's scholarship fund to grow from $4.8 million the year before the AT&T Center opened to $7.2 million in 2006. The fund now benefits 3,000 Texas students from 153 counties. The AT&T Center has also helped attract more Mexican cattlemen and vaqueros. With its increased funding, SALE has set up an annual scholarship presentation to the Coahuila and Nuevo León cattlemen's associations.

With increased revenues from the arena, SALE in 2005 brought in the best stock for the rodeo. It also limited the number of contestants to the top seventy-two money winners from the professional associations' best for each event. This was equivalent to replacing a minor league baseball team with a major league team. The rodeo now features the best stock and top-ranked contestants, and it has become one of the first stops for professional cowboys and cow-girls who compete to appear in the Wrangler Rodeo Finals in Las Vegas. It is one of the nation's top five rodeos and is ranked third in prize money awarded during the regular season.

This new status led the rodeo to be recognized nationally. In December 2005 Keith Martin, SALE's executive director, accepted an award for Best Large Indoor Rodeo of the Year from the Professional Rodeo Cowboys Association. The rodeo has an estimated $100 million impact on our community, drawing thousands of tourists to the city.

Twelve trail rides that come to San Antonio during the rodeo have increased in attendance. Originating from small cities throughout South and Central Texas, the rides represent the history of ranching, cattle drives, and horsemanship. The Old Chisholm, South Texas, Laredo, La Grande, Six Flags, Texas, Mesquite, Hill Country, Alamo, Cowboy, Kerr County, and Greater Randolph Area trail rides all converge at the AT&T Center.

The rodeo's success has led to planning for an equestrian center that will bring up to eighteen major horse events to San Antonio. It also led to planning a restoration of the coliseum to create additional exhibit halls. During the rodeo the coliseum serves as exhibit space for retailers of Western wear, furniture, and other items. Finally, the rodeo's success has increased the popularity of Western art in San Antonio. Collectors Jack Guenther, Mark Watson, and John Montford are leading an effort to create the Dolph and Janey Briscoe Western Art Museum in the old Hertzberg Museum downtown. Former Governor Briscoe has donated $4 million to the museum.

The Stock Show & Rodeo will continue to grow in importance as it solidifies its position as the nation's best indoor rodeo.

RAILROADS

Approximately eighty trains averaging 100 freight cars go through San Antonio daily. Seventy percent of the trains carry pass-through freight. According to a study conducted by the county, rail freight tonnage in the area will double by 2025. We do not have the rail lines, however, to accommodate that.

San Antonio's influence with the railroads has always been minimal because none of the railroad's larger shippers were based here. The Toyota plant gave us the power to persuade Union Pacific to work with us on a number of critical rail issues. A series of accidents that began in 2004 made clear the strains of our inadequate rail track. Early on the morning of June 28, 2004, Carl Mixon, Bexar County's emergency director, called to tell me that at 5:03 A.M. a westbound Union Pacific train had run into an eastbound Burlington Northern train in southwest Bexar County. A tanker car of liquefied chlorine gas had ruptured. Four people died as a result of the wreck.

After going to the site, I met with Union Pacific President Jim Turner in my office. "With the increase in rail freight going through our city, we're going to see more accidents," I told him. "We must address rail relocation as well as safety on existing tracks. Relocating at least one of your two rail yards out of the inner city also would help."

"We've been successful with rail relocation in Denver, Chicago, and Reno," Turner said, adding that he would send a team of

Union Pacific officials to meet with me. Less than three weeks later we met at the courthouse with Union Pacific representatives Scott Moore and Joe Adams; Rep. Mike Krusee, chairman of the House Transportation Committee; Tullos Wells, chairman of the Austin–San Antonio Intermunicipal Commuter Rail District; City Councilman Richard Perez; Robert Nichols, Texas Department of Transportation commissioner; Bruce Flohr, chairman of the Bexar County Rail District; and Mike Novak, former commissioner and chairman of the Greater San Antonio Chamber of Commerce. Also attending were several congressmen and representatives from VIA and KellyUSA.

We agreed to work with Union Pacific on moving their intermodal rail yard out of a populated area on the West Side near KellyUSA. This would reduce inner-city truck and rail traffic. The fact that Toyota was locating on the South Side was a driving force in the decision. Union Pacific agreed to step up rail safety measures. We also agreed to begin a $500,000 study on routes that could divert rail traffic to a new line that would loop southeast around the city.

Three more accidents occurred between September and November. In the third one, on November 11, a train ran into a Crystal Cold Storage building, killing one person. Six days later I was on my way to Washington to personally appeal for help on rail safety issues. Garza and I met with U.S. senators Kay Bailey Hutchison and John Cornyn; Congressmen Ciro Rodriguez and Charlie Gonzalez; and Kirk Van Tine, deputy secretary of the U.S. Department of Transportation. As a result the Federal Railroad Administration, a division of the Department of Transportation, stepped up its enforcement. Toyota officials also let it be known they expected a better safety record from Union Pacific. Toyota was serious about safety. It had shut down construction on its plant when too many accidents occurred. Union Pacific had to listen to Toyota because the company was one of the railroad's largest customers.

Seth Mitchell, my chief of staff; Leilah Powell, my government relations manager; and I traveled to Fort Worth, the national headquarters of Burlington Northern Santa Fe Corp., to meet with CEO Matt Rose. At a conference table with several Burlington officials, Rose said: "If freight business keeps growing as expected, we'll need $10 billion a year for ten years for new rail line construction. Somehow we have to convince Congress that it needs to participate financially. Taking more freight off the highways would save money in highway construction for the government. Large trucks carrying freight are a lot more dangerous than rail freight." When I suggested we needed something like what President Eisenhower did for the highways in the 1950s, Rose agreed. I told him I was participating in a statewide planning group on rail relocation, and hopefully the state would take the lead.

After much behind-the-scenes work, Union Pacific CEO Dick Davidson came to San Antonio in March 2005 to sign a historic memorandum of understanding with Governor Perry that would provide a public-private partnership to relocate rail lines. At a press conference Davidson added a little levity by saying he was spurred to action because "I've had a wolf at my neck for the last year."

In response to the governor's initiative, the Texas legislature authorized submission to the voters of a constitutional amendment to set up a rail relocation fund. At a press conference in October, Rep. Ruth Jones McClendon, Hardberger, and I urged people to vote for Proposition 1 on the November ballot. After voters approved the amendment, work began to encourage the next session of the legislature to fund the measure.

The issue was critical to the Austin–San Antonio corridor. A proposed 122-mile rail route would be located east of IH-35, running from Taylor, north of Austin, to San Antonio at a cost of approximately $1.8 billion. All pass-through freight would be moved from the corridor to the new rail line. The 2007 legislature provided access to funding for rail relocation from the Texas Emissions Reduction Plan, a fund that contains more than $100 million.

Rail safety began to improve in San Antonio after Union Pacific invested millions of dollars in rail improvements, additional personnel, and enhanced safety training. In March 2006 the Federal Rail Administration reported that accidents were down from 25 to 18, and fatalities were down from 4 to 0.

We also worked with Union Pacific to build a $100 million dollar multimodal terminal on 300 acres of land south of town, between Loop 410 and Loop 1604 off Old Pearsall Road. The terminal would be critical to reduce rail and truck traffic in the heart of San Antonio and to connect with a proposed new rail loop around south Bexar County. Less rail traffic and 80,000 fewer trucks would enter the city, and the terminal would provide support of the Toyota plant and the opportunity for distribution businesses to locate near it. We worked with Southwest

Independent School District officials to assure that safety and environmental issues were addressed. In August 2007 I attended the groundbreaking for Union Pacific's multimodal yard.

Were it not for Toyota's location here, we could not have made progress on these issues. It gave us leverage with Union Pacific and the state. While much remains to be done, we are off to a good start.

THE ENVIRONMENT

During the highly charged debate over the PGA Village, its opponents refused to acknowledge the significant environmental protections that were negotiated between city officials and Lumbermen's. The project will develop under the most extensive, restrictive environmental standards in the state.

Lumbermen's donated more than 790 acres of land for open space and conservation easements. Another 600 acres set aside for the two golf courses must be certified through the Audubon Cooperative Sanctuary Program by Audubon International. Several TPC golf courses elsewhere are located in the country's top ten master-planned communities. The two courses are required to construct a retention/closed loop irrigation system that must capture a minimum of 85 percent of the golf course irrigated area. The courses also must use twelve-inch clay containment on top of the soil and meet a water pollution abatement plan approved by the San Antonio Water System.

When Lumbermen's accepted a 15 percent impervious cover restriction, the company set a new standard for development over the city's aquifer recharge zone. With 85 percent of the property not covered over, the PGA Village will be used as a benchmark for any development agreement over the recharge zone that includes financial support from the city or county.

Public improvement district board members appointed by Commissioners Court will monitor the agreements. The San Antonio Water System will receive $100,000 annually from the district to monitor the water pollution abatement provisions.

Lumbermen's has gone beyond the agreement's requirements by installing water-sensitive landscaping along the boulevard leading into the development, as well as in the yards of homes. The developer is installing a drip irrigation system for the homes and public landscaping, and it will build a series of hiking trails connecting to a community center. This will increase our standing as one of the nation's best walking cities. In 2003 *Prevention* magazine and the American Podiatric Medical Association named San Antonio one of the country's top twelve cities for walking, citing our air quality, 157 miles of natural creekways, and varied topography.

The PGA Village has set a higher standard for the city's future developments. Even so, there is the continuing need to seek additional environmental safeguards.

PUBLIC IMPROVEMENT DISTRICTS

When we successfully lobbied the Texas legislature for Bexar County to create a public improvement district for the PGA Village, the legislature granted us the authority to create other districts. No other county in the state has the authority to create what amounted to a semi-city government.

The authority could not have come at a better time. In 1999 the legislature restricted cities' power to annex, requiring them to give a three-year notice and develop a comprehensive plan to serve the annexed area. Before these restrictions, cities had enjoyed unencumbered power to annex. San Antonio had an aggressive annexation plan that made it the nation's seventh-largest city. In the last few years very little territory, with the exception of the area around the Toyota plant, has been annexed.

A public improvement district, which can be created by the county, provides the opportunity to access the same taxes as the City of San Antonio. When population begins to increase in an area of the county, the demand for services also increases, often beyond the capacity of the county's limited tax authority to provide those services. If the city does not annex the area, a public improvement district becomes necessary.

As I mentioned earlier, we created a district not only for the PGA Village but also for the South Side. We have created a third one on the West Side between Potranco and Culebra roads. I am sure more are to come.

The four initiatives—the AT&T Center, Toyota, the PGA Village, and the San Antonio River Walk extension—have had a major impact on our community. But for that impact to be sustained, we must build on them and plan for future investments.

SIX

· ·

The Next Level

WITH ITS FOUR BUILDING BLOCKS, San Antonio is taking an economic and cultural leap forward. Collectively and individually, these projects have set the city on a path into the upper ranks of American cities. And because the city is experiencing the best of times and our economy is producing high income in both the private and public sectors, we have the resources to invest in our future. But we must demonstrate that we have the community leadership to make the investments that will enable us to move to the next level.

Doing so will require public and private partnerships and will call for a new generation of business and civic leaders to become active participants and investors. It will require city and county officials to provide public funds to match private investments. To sustain the momentum, we must make these investments now and into the next decade.

The city and county must act to determine the next big public investments. It has been said that vision without resources is a hallucination. If we are going to look forward to new investments we need to identify a funding source. One source that has produced revenues beyond expectation is the hotel-motel tax. When the county financed the AT&T Center with bonds secured by the hotel-motel tax and a car rental tax, the estimate was that it would take twenty years to pay off the bonds. But because of new hotels and increased rental of existing hotel rooms, tax revenue grew more quickly than the county's very conservative estimates. In 2006 San Antonio ranked first in the nation in the percentage of room night increases, and by 2007 more hotels were being built here than in any other American city. In summer 2005 David Smith, the county's budget director, projected that we would pay off the AT&T Center debt as early as 2012, instead of 2020. We could refinance our debt before 2012, providing over $300 million for projects.

The legislation that allowed the arena to be built with the visitor tax provided that it could be used for other projects as well, such as a tourist development area along an inland waterway— that is, the San Antonio River or municipal parks and recreation, a convention center facility, or an opera house, theater, music hall, zoological park, museum, or sports venue. If commissioners decided to refinance the bonds, we could make another major investment.

Before we could consider other projects, a hurricane blew an investment opportunity our way. When Hurricane Katrina hit New Orleans in August 2005, thousands of evacuees made their way to San Antonio. One famous evacuee was Tom Benson, owner of the New Orleans Saints. Although he was a native of New Orleans, he had lived in San Antonio, where he owned a bank and several car dealerships. With the New Orleans dome incapacitated, he told

Mayor Phil Hardberger he wanted the Saints to play their 2005 season in San Antonio. Many doubted that New Orleans would ever recover, and hence the team might move to San Antonio. We had the opportunity to prove to the NFL and to Benson that we would draw large crowds to the games.

While I was enthusiastic, I had doubts about our chances. During my term as mayor in the early 1990s, the NFL had decided to grant two new expansion franchises. With the Alamodome under construction, we thought we were ready for a team. Tom Benson's brother, Larry, who practices law in San Antonio, told me he would put up the $100,000 NFL application fee. He backed out at the last minute, and I convinced Red McCombs to put up the fee. After McCombs and I made a presentation to NFL officials in New York, San Antonio did not even make the short list. We later learned that Larry Benson had written NFL officials a letter that was critical of McCombs.

Putting aside that unpleasant memory, I worked with Hardberger to create a leadership group to ensure that Saints games in San Antonio would be a success. Councilmen Chip Haass and Kevin Wolff, AT&T executive John Montford, Greater Chamber president Joe Krier, and former mayor Henry Cisneros were charged with planning an initiative to promote sponsorships and tickets to the business community. In September the leadership group met for breakfast in the Dominion Country Club boardroom to plan our strategy.

Hardberger opened the meeting, saying, "I met this week with Tom. He said they could play up to five games this season. But most important, he told me he wants the Saints to move here permanently." Cisneros said, "I've talked to top NFL officials and told them this is a different city from ten years ago. But they're sensitive about the New Orleans crisis. They want the Saints to play some games in Baton Rouge. I'm not sure they'll consider a permanent move at this time." By the end of breakfast, we agreed we would concentrate on selling out the games and not engage in efforts to move the team here permanently. We set a date for a large gathering of business leaders where we would promote ticket and sponsorship sales.

NFL Commissioner Paul Tagliabue made things difficult by granting us only three games, the last on Christmas Eve, a challenging date to sell out a game. This was not a good signal about a possible permanent move of the Saints. Nevertheless we had a successful rally with the business community and sold several blocks of tickets and suites. When tickets went on sale to the general public, hundreds lined up as early as 4 A.M. to purchase them. In the first two days fans purchased 85,000 tickets for the three games.

More than 50,000 people attended the first game at the Alamodome on October 2, cheering as the Saints beat the Buffalo Bills 19–7. Afterward a beaming Benson thanked us all for helping. Ten days later at a leadership group meeting, Cisneros reported that Benson had told him he wanted the Saints to relocate here permanently.

With the funding capacity from the venue tax, the county had the financial ability to restore and improve the Alamodome to meet NFL standards. In 2000 a Marmon Mok and HOK Sports study found that the dome's 38 suites could be enlarged to 104 and that club seats could expand from 5,000 to 6,700. We would have to build a $20 million training facility and provide additional parking. Making these changes and bringing the dome up to the standards of other NFL stadiums would require between $106 and $136 million.

The Saints played their second game on October 16 to a full house of 65,562 fans. After the game Hardberger told *San Antonio Express-News* reporter Tom Orsborn that he would actively pursue the Saints' permanent move. But that effort quickly blew up when Tagliabue announced that the NFL would not support it. Even with the negative statement from the NFL commissioner, more than 60,000 fans showed up on Christmas Eve for the third and final game.

In January 2006 Tagliabue visited with Benson in San Antonio. After the meeting Benson announced that the Saints would play their 2006 games in Louisiana. Tagliabue made no effort to talk to Hardberger or me. The NFL attitude had not changed since our failure to obtain a franchise in 1992. A few days later Tagliabue and Benson had a press conference in New Orleans. The commissioner said Benson was committed to keeping the Saints in New Orleans beyond the 2006 season, and Benson confirmed the statement. The state of Louisiana and the city of New Orleans were investing substantial funds into repairing their dome.

For the time being, San Antonio's next investment was not going to be an NFL franchise. We should have learned a valuable lesson: Be sure the commissioner and the team owner are on the same page. Be leery of a team owner who may be trying to play your city against his team's home.

But we didn't learn the lesson, or at least I didn't. In November 2005 I had received a call from John McHale Jr., Major League Baseball's vice president, who told me Florida Marlins President David Samson wanted to come to San Antonio. "He may relocate the team to another city because it's last in attendance," he said, "and he can't get Miami to help build a new stadium." This was the case even though the Marlins had won the World Series in 1997 and 2003.

Baseball is my game. The 6,500-seat Texas League stadium where the San Antonio Missions play is named after me. I wrote a book on the sport, *Baseball for Real Men*, and I still play hardball in the Men's Senior Baseball League. If not NFL football, why not focus on Major League Baseball?

In December Samson and two of his staff arrived in San Antonio. Hardberger, District Attorney Susan Reed, and I presented a plan to fund up to $200 million to build a new stadium. The Marlins group later visited several other potential relocation cities.

Samson called in mid-February and said, "I just want you to know we're going to relocate. We're in the process of assessing your market. I want to meet with you sooner rather than later." I took him at his word and spent a great deal of time lining up potential team investors, including McCombs, Cisneros, and Nolan Ryan. I convinced several companies to commit to advertising and tickets.

Citizens began to get excited about a possible Marlins relocation. WOAI commissioned a poll showing that 71 percent supported bringing Major League Baseball to San Antonio. A radio poll showed that 52 percent supported building a stadium with the hotel-motel tax.

On March 2 the *Miami Herald* reported that, according to Bob DuPuy, Major League Baseball president, San Antonio had become the focus of the Marlins' relocation discussions. This was the president of the league speaking, not just an owner. Baseball guys are different. You can trust them. I am one of them. The next level for San Antonio was going to be Major League Baseball.

Samson called on March 14 and said, "It's going to take us two weeks or longer to assess the stadium proposal, a media package for broadcast of the games, and economic data on San Antonio. We need to be sure Major League Baseball agrees with our assessment. If that report is favorable, I want to come to San Antonio and not leave until we have a deal."

A red flag flashed across my frontal lobe—the delay and provisos sounded fishy. I told Samson I was disappointed in the delay and that I could not hold the offer open past May 15. While there was nothing special about the date, I was not going to play this game indefinitely. I followed up with a letter stating that the Marlins needed to fish or cut bait by May 15.

The next day the *Express-News* endorsed the effort to attract the Marlins, writing, "Like a kid fidgeting on the bench, San Antonio is ready—no, eager—to play."

Hardberger, Reed, and I traveled to Houston on April 3 at the invitation of Samson and his stepfather, Jeffrey Loria, owner of the Marlins, to watch the team's opening game against the Astros. It was a nice visit, filled with small talk, as we watched a good ballgame.

As we traveled home I received a call from DuPuy. "I realize you're under time constraints," he said. "We'll focus on San Antonio and try to complete our work by May 15." He called again a few days later to say that the league was having a hard time deciding whether to give up its strategic plan to have baseball in southern Florida.

Samson called a few days before the deadline and asked me to extend it. I refused. After the deadline expired I received a letter from DuPuy saying, "We are not in a position to affirmatively approve the relocation of the Marlins to San Antonio right now . . . the work you have done will not be in vain, since you will have positioned your city to be strongly considered for a future Major League Baseball team."

I had spent more than four months on the effort only to find out that baseball guys are no more trustworthy than football guys. Today the Marlins are still last or next-to-last in league attendance, and they still do not have a stadium. I hope they are having fun.

Although pursuit of the Saints and the Marlins did not cost the city or county any money, Hardberger and I put a lot of work into it. Did we compromise our city in some way by making the two failed efforts, or did we position San Antonio for a major league franchise somewhere down the road? We probably will not know until after Hardberger and I are off the stage.

If the next level for San Antonio was not the NFL or MLB, what then? After the Marlins and the Saints headed back to the shores of Florida and Louisiana, I had time to take a deep breath and think things through. Several needs in our community could be funded by the visitor tax.

The San Antonio Sports Foundation had been working on a twenty-year plan to build regional sports complexes that would benefit our citizens and bring amateur sporting events to San Antonio. The 2002 Arts Collaborative I co-chaired with Garza concluded that we needed a performing arts center. San Antonio was the only city its size that did not have one. A study in the 2003 edition of *Historic/Cultural Traveler* found that 81 percent of U.S. adults who travel are considered historic/cultural travelers, and 30 percent of them say a specific historic or cultural event influences their choice of destination. They stay seven nights or longer and spend more money than the average visitor who stays three nights. We still needed additional funds to complete the thirteen-mile river extension, and we needed to establish a fund to renovate the AT&T Center when it reaches the age of fifteen to twenty years. A fund for the Alamodome had not been established, and as a result it was no longer a state-of-the-art dome.

I began to visit with various groups to see if they were interested in Commissioners Court taking up these issues and submitting them to the voters for their consideration. I met with Milton Guess and several members of the San Antonio Hotel and Lodging Association who supported using the visitor tax for the San Antonio River. I met with Susan Blackwood, the president of the San Antonio Sports Foundation, who said they were about to complete their plan and supported taking the proposition of regional sports complexes to the voters.

I met with Felix Padrón, director of the city's Office of Cultural Affairs. I had worked with him on the 2002 Arts Collaborative, in which over 1,000 people participated in interviews, focus groups, and community forums. The 2005 final report, which was adopted by the city council, contained thirty-eight strategies. Padrón agreed to work with us on promoting the most important recommendation—to build a performing arts center.

Padrón had funded a study by ArtsMarket, Inc., which found that local performing arts groups, including the San Antonio Symphony, Lyric Opera, Metropolitan Ballet, Arts San Antonio, Cactus Pear Music Festival, Youth Orchestras, and Magik Theatre, needed a state-of-the-art performing arts center. Since 1989 the San Antonio Symphony had been playing in the restored Majestic Theater, which did not have good acoustics and was managed by a for-profit company that gave date preferences to touring productions. The other local performing groups played in other venues that were costly and inadequate.

I knew we were sailing into uncharted waters. No Texas county or city had ever sought to use the hotel-motel and car rental taxes to fund such a diversity of projects. Voters were usually given a choice to build only a professional sports stadium, but we had a rare opportunity to give them a chance to support projects that would benefit them as well as the tourism industry. The San Antonio River project would be the least problematic since a plan was already in place. Voters would be reluctant to approve additional funds for the AT&T Center, though, and we faced a major challenge with the performing arts center since we had no location. I knew various sports facilities would be proposed, resulting in a difficult choice for the task force.

By fall 2006 I was ready to go, but I needed someone who had experience and could devote their full time to the task. Mike

Sculley, husband of City Manager Sheryl Sculley, fit the bill. He had been president of the Maricopa County Sports Commission while his wife was working for the City of Phoenix. He had experience putting together plans for several sporting venues using the visitor tax. He was doing consultant work for the San Antonio Sports Foundation. I talked to him, and he agreed to work with the county as a consultant. Commissioners Court approved his contract in December. I received some criticism from the media because I did not put out a proposal request and because Sculley was the city manager's husband. I stated that he was uniquely qualified for the job and I did not want to hire anyone else.

We assembled a county team made up of Seth Mitchell, my chief of staff, and Clay Chrisman, his assistant; Budget Director David Smith; and Special Projects Administrator Cindy Segovia. Working with Mike Sculley, we decided to create three task forces: culture facilities, amateur sports facilities, and the San Antonio River. Commissioners Court, the Community Arenas Board, SALE, and the Spurs would continue to work on plans for the coliseum grounds and the arena. Sculley presented the process to Commissioners Court, and the court agreed to move forward.

Over the next several weeks the court came up with a list of more than sixty citizens who were willing to serve on one of the task forces. We received solicited recommendations from chambers of commerce, arts organizations, amateur sports organizations, and other groups. In early May 2007 Sculley requested the court's approval of members of the three task forces. He also requested that each task force be allocated 25 percent of the tax's proceeds, with 25 percent remaining for the arena and coliseum grounds. This was an estimated $75 million for each task force. Each was responsible for assessing community interest and building a consensus for development of venue projects as defined by the authorizing legislation. Each would report to the court by January 2008. The court unanimously agreed to move forward.

The task forces had approximately twenty members each. It was important that a chair and vice chair be selected that had the time, expertise, political connections, and passion to get the job done. I carefully selected the six I thought would do the best job and could garner the necessary political support for the initiatives. I wanted a chair or vice chair to come from the tourist industry. I did not want the Hotel and Lodging Association fighting this vote as they had on the Spurs arena. I asked Marco Barrios, executive director of the San Antonio Area Tourism Council, and George Block, assistant director of athletics for Northside Independent School District, to be chair and vice chair respectively of the Amateur Sports Facilities task force. Both were also board members of the San Antonio Sports Foundation. Former Councilman Richard Perez and Milton Guess, secretary-treasurer of the Tourism Council, agreed to act as chair and vice chair respectively of the River Walk extension task force. Symphony Chairperson Debbie Montford and hotelier Henry Feldman took on the task of chair and vice chair respectively of the Culture Facilities task force.

Our county team met with all six leaders at the San Antonio Sports Foundation offices in the Alamodome. Sculley presented the proposed criteria for selecting each task force's projects. We carefully planned the first meeting of each task force and developed a timeline of meetings over the next few months. Each task force would be given a comprehensive legal briefing.

I attended the first task force meetings on July 10, 11, and 12 and recommended the chairs and vice chairs, whom the task forces voted affirmatively to accept. The San Antonio Sports Foundation provided staffing for the Amateur Sports Facilities task force. The San Antonio River Authority staffed the River Walk extension task force. The city's Office of Cultural Affairs staffed the Culture Facilities task force. Each task force was briefed on the legal issues, their responsibilities, and the timeline required to give Commissioners Court a recommendation in December. The court would vote by January 8 to submit the proposed ballot language to the attorney general for his approval. The election would have to be called in February.

As the task forces began their work I met with Commissioner Paul Elizondo, Spurs officials Leo Gomez and Rick Pych, San Antonio Stock Show & Rodeo officials Tom Frost and Keith Martin, and members of the Coliseum Advisory Board—all of whom were ready to develop a plan to take to the voters. I asked Elizondo to take the lead on behalf of the court in negotiating a plan. I also asked Pych if the Spurs would conduct a poll on the issues. He agreed to employ Baselice and Associates, the consulting firm that had polled for the Spurs during the arena campaign. I asked Trish DeBerry to run the campaign, and she agreed. I had worked with her on several campaigns, and her public relations firm is one of the best in the city.

At the end of July I met with DeBerry, Michael Baselice, and

Gomez at DeBerry's office to receive Baselice's poll briefing. The voters supported three of the issues, with at least 60 percent of those polled in favor. Renovation funds for the AT&T Center, however, received support from just over 51 percent.

A month later the *Express-News* broke a front page story on the proposed fund to renovate the AT&T Center. Several sources said the Spurs should pay for the upgrades. Four NBA championships may have hurt the chances of voter approval; many citizens considered the team successful enough to pay for it themselves. Radio talk shows badgered the idea. We faced the task of explaining to voters that Bexar County taxpayers owned the building and that the Spurs were paying rent and had already invested $64 million in the arena.

In mid-September the University of Texas at San Antonio (UTSA) student body voted 3,031 to 1,571 to double their athletic fees, allowing the university to improve their sixteen sports programs and to field a football team with the hope of reaching the Division 1-A conference within ten years. Schools like Rice University, Southern Methodist University, Tulane University, and the University of Houston are in the conference. One of the requirements to enter Division 1-A is for a university to have first-class sports fields and facilities, including a football field. The vote was significant in encouraging the Amateur Sports Facilities task force to support the sports complex UTSA wanted to build. The sports complex would be open for use by local high schools, youth athletic clubs, and other amateur sports organizations.

As information seeped out about the poll results, *Express-News* columnist Roddy Stinson called me. I admitted that there was a poll and gave him the rough numbers, but I did not tell him who paid for it. He called Gomez, who told him the Spurs paid for the poll. Stinson wrote a generally favorable article that included the poll results. If Gomez and I had clammed up, he would have written a nasty column.

In early August I called Ken Halliday with Silver Ventures, the developers of Pearl Brewery, to see if they would be interested in housing the performing arts center in their development. He said they were and suggested that we visit the Bass Performing Arts Center in Fort Worth. On August 13 Halliday, Debbie Montford, Tobin Endowment president Bruce Bugg, Darryl Byrd, and I flew to Fort Worth on Silver Ventures' private plane to meet with Paul Beard, managing director of the Bass center.

We spent several hours with Beard touring the facility and learning about the theater's operation. The facility, which was built in 1998 for $72 million, had the best of acoustics for nonamplified music and the ability to convert for amplification performances. While local performing arts groups had priority, Beard also booked Broadway shows and touring artists that were profitable and enabled him to subsidize the local groups. He said he hosted 300 event nights a year in the multipurpose theater, which had sparked a revival of downtown.

Based on Beard's recommendation, Commissioners Court hired Bud Franks to develop a business plan for a performing arts center. An expert in the field, he had developed plans for the Hobby Center for the Performing Arts, and the Broadway Center for the Performing arts, as well as several other music halls.

Debbie Montford had created a task force on financing and

appointed Bugg as chairman. Bugg, along with Leroy Denman, is a trustee of the $100 million Tobin Endowment. Robert Tobin, who passed away in April 2002, left his fortune to the endowment. An ardent supporter of the performing arts, he served on the board of directors for the Metropolitan Opera in New York. Bugg wasted no time creating a nonprofit foundation to raise private funds for the performing arts center, which we decided to call the Bexar County Performing Arts Foundation. Bugg, Reed, Hardberger, Montford, and I acted as the incorporators.

In September Montford and I met with architect Stefanos Polyzoides, the lead architect drafting a plan for 194 acres on the River North project. He envisioned a theater district that stretched from Municipal Auditorium down Third Street a few blocks to the Scottish Rite Temple. He believed Municipal Auditorium could be converted into a first-class performing arts center.

The 1926 iconic façade building was built as a memorial to World War I veterans. A 1979 fire gutted the interior, which was restored in 1985. The large auditorium provided seating for 4,800; two other rooms could seat up to 125 for musical recitals. The building backs up to the San Antonio River just south of Lexington Avenue where the two-mile river improvement project was under way.

I asked Hardberger if he would consider making the auditorium available, and he said he would. Montford and I met with City Manager Sculley, who also liked the idea. It was booked for only eighty events a year, which required the city to subsidize its operation with $500,000 a year. We asked Sculley to include the adjoining 1926 fire department building, which could be used for offices and a possible rehearsal hall. She said she would consider it since the fire department was planning to move.

City staff led by Assistant City Manager Penny Postoak-Ferguson and Mike Sawaya, convention, sports, and entertainment facilities director, drafted a staff report recommending three city sites: Municipal Auditorium and the fire department building, a HemisFair site, and the Lila Cockrell Theater in the convention center. They ranked Municipal Auditorium as their first choice.

Montford had appointed Elisa Chan to chair a subcommittee analyzing the possible sites. We toured Municipal Auditorium along with members of her task force, and after the tour we had a briefing from architect Michael Guarino of Ford Powell & Carson showing that a 2,400-seat theater and a second, smaller theater could be built within the facility. Guarino had been an architect on the project converting the Palmer Auditorium in Austin into the Long Center for the Performing Arts. *Express-News* reporter Tracy Hamilton joined the tour and wrote a front page story.

Subsequent to the tour I received a call from Ken Halliday, who said that a site at Pearl Brewery would not be offered.

On November 2 Montford and I attended a briefing of the Municipal Auditorium staff recommendation to the city council. The mayor and council members spoke in favor, save Lourdes Galvan. The vote was delayed until the following Monday, which gave Galvan time to round up a group that asked the council to delay the vote once again. She was not able to get a second to her motion, and the staff recommendation passed 9–1.

In addition to the city's proposed sites, Montford's task force received two others, from UTSA for a site next to the downtown campus and from Henry Muñoz, who proposed the Alameda Theater. Hardberger and I had a private breakfast at El Mirador on November 8. After going over the sites, we agreed that Municipal Auditorium was our best choice. It had great political appeal. We would restore a historic building and at the same time build a performance hall inside. It was located on the river and would lead to further development in the area. We would not be creating another venue that would compete with Municipal. It might even be less expensive. And we felt the voters would be more inclined to support a proposition where the county and city were working together and sharing resources.

Chan, Montford, and I met with a team of experts who had toured all five sites and the Majestic Theatre. They were acoustic and audio expert Mark Holden with Jaffe Holden, based in Santa Monica, California; design and construction expert Chris Kay with the Irvine team, based in Houston; theater planning and design expert Joseph Mobilia with Fisher Dachs Associates, based in New York; and Bud Franks. Holden said, "You want to create a flexible, intimate music hall with acoustics that create a rich warm vibration and transport the audience into the music world. You do not have such an acoustic gem in San Antonio."

They worked up a matrix on all five sites to present to Chan's committee. The consensus was that Municipal Auditorium offered the best opportunity to create a first-rate theater. The stage was large enough for opera and for the symphony and had the proper height—seventy feet. The rest of the roof, at forty feet, would have to be raised to provide the proper acoustics and bring the balcony closer. The auditorium also had room for small theater that would seat 200, as well as a rehearsal hall.

Meanwhile the proposed fund for the arena came under attack when a front page headline in the *Express-News* read, "An Arena wasteland, AT&T Center has failed to revive east side." While the story was fairly well balanced, the headline insinuated that the arena had created a wasteland. It took fifteen years to create development around the Alamodome, and the arena had been in place just five years.

After many months of hard work, all three task forces reported their recommendations over a three-day period. On December 4 the Amateur Sports Facilities task force voted unanimously to recommend thirteen of the nineteen proposals they had received. The proposals reflected facilities located throughout the county, with the UTSA sports complex and the Mission Concepcíon sports complex receiving the largest share of the funding—$10 million and $16.1 million respectively. The total impact on the county's sports facilities would add forty-six soccer fields, doubling our tournament capacity, and would provide the only basketball and volleyball indoor tournament facility under one roof, as well as twenty-one youth and ten regulation-size baseball diamonds, twenty-two softball diamonds, the only swimming stadium in the central United States, seven football fields, three tracks, one cross country course, and a dedicated fencing facility.

The next day the San Antonio River task force recommended $125 million in funding, prioritizing the first $75 million in case Commissioners Court did not approve the full amount. The task force allocated $81.25 million for trails, footbridges, portals to the missions, landscaping, and artwork along the Mission Reach, as well as funds for completion of the Museum Reach to Brackenridge Park, including trails, bridges, crossings, landscaping, and fencing.

The Culture Facilities task force on December 6 recommended $110 million in funding to renovate Municipal Auditorium into a performing arts center, to include a 2,000-seat theater, a 250–450-seat studio theater, a rehearsal hall, and a veterans memorial plaza. On Hardberger's recommendation the task force also included a memorial for Medal of Honor recipients from the San Antonio area. This would complement the existing memorials for veterans of the Korean and Vietnam Wars.

On December 13 the three task forces held an information session at Municipal Auditorium. Commissioners Court ran an ad announcing the briefing, and about 300 people—all supporters of the various projects—attended. It was a good sign that no organized opposition showed up.

A few days later the court heard reports from the task force chairs and from Bexar County Executive Director David Marquez, whom Commissioner Elizondo had appointed to lead the staff negotiations with SALE, the Spurs, and the Community Arenas Board. Marquez reported that the parties had agreed to a $75 million investment in the arena to upgrade seating, technology, energy efficiency, and aesthetic improvements. The Spurs would extend their lease by five years and invest an additional $15 million in the arena; they would also be responsible for any cost overruns. An additional $15 million would be used to replace SALE barns with multipurpose agriculture exhibit space. SALE would invest

$2.4 million, and $10 million would be allocated for renovating the coliseum to replace lower seating with retractable seats, replace the mechanical system, and make aesthetic improvements.

After the presentation Elizondo moved to add two other projects. He convinced the court to fund $4 million for the Dolph and Janey Briscoe Western Art Museum. The building would also include a San Antonio history center. The National Western Art Foundation and the city and county were partners on the project. The court also approved Elizondo's motion to include $6 million for restoring the Alameda Theater.

The court then instructed David Smith to come up with a financing plan that included $125 million for the river; $105 million for the performing arts; $75 million for sports facilities; $100 million for the arena, barns, and coliseum; and $10 million for the Western art museum and the Alameda Theater. The total was $415 million. Smith had already begun work on the expanded budget several weeks earlier, after it became apparent that the task force recommendations would require a higher level of spending to meet the budget's projected needs

Elizondo, Smith, Seth Mitchell, and I met for breakfast at El Mirador on December 28. Smith presented a draft of his financial plan. He recommended issuing $415 million in bonds that would be staggered over a six-year period. The bonds would be issued for a thirty-four-year period based on a conservative growth rate in the visitor tax. If hotel-motel and car rental revenue increases continued as they had over the last twenty years, the bonds would be paid off in twenty to twenty-five years—that is, as many as fourteen years early.

A few days later the court held a hearing on the Alameda Theater and the Western Art Museum, followed by a public hearing at which about thirty people spoke. After a financial briefing from Smith we approved the $415 million with only one change: we diverted $5 million from the performing arts center to the UTSA sports complex. The vote was unanimous.

The following day I met with DeBerry and our campaign team to begin work. We chose some twenty civic leaders to be part of a team that would meet weekly and scheduled our first meeting for the next week.

In the previous few months we had pressed the attorney general for direction on whether the ballot should be presented to voters in one vote or four. While I preferred one vote, I mainly wanted an answer because it would affect how we ran the campaign. On January 8, as I was having lunch with Bugg and Frost at Club Giraud, District Attorney Susan Reed called to say that the attorney general had ruled that there should be four separate votes. At the court meeting that afternoon we instructed staff to prepare four ballot propositions and submit the package, and the next week the court voted to submit the propositions.

As this book goes to press, we do not know the outcome of the May vote. If voters approve the four proposals, it will be another major step in San Antonio's evolution toward a world-class city. Bond approval will have a significant impact on our quality of life, enhancing arts and culture, establishing the city as an amateur sports capital, completing the San Antonio River Walk extension, and improving the community arenas. It will lay the groundwork for a better city for our children, grandchildren, and the generations to come.

There are, of course, numerous other projects to complete and other investments essential to building a thriving community. The city needs to complete the $500 million bond program that voters approved under Hardberger's leadership in 2007 for streets, drainage, parks, and libraries. The county must begin construction— and finish within ten years—on the $500 million bond flood control plan the court authorized in 2007. The court needs to approve $700 million for hospital beds and an expanded trauma care facility for the Bexar County Hospital District. The state must find funds to finance and build additional freeways in our area. Our metropolitan transit system should step up and build San Antonio's first light-rail system for passenger service. The state and local school districts need to substantially improve our public education system—and that does not necessarily mean spending more money. The Alamo Community College District and our five major colleges and universities must continue to expand in order to meet their growing student population.

Our city will continue to progress if we have the willpower and determination to make the investments for a better tomorrow. I believe we do.

INDEX

Aceves, Joe, 6, 160

Adams, Joe, 202

Adkisson, Tommy, 43, 44, 45, 119–20,
    152–53, 155, 163, 171

Agnese, Lou, 127

Aguilar, Al, 190

Ahrens, John, 141

Alameda Theater, 136, 228

Alamo, 128, 137

Alamo Community College District,
    187

Alamo Iron Works, 15

Alamo National Bank Building,
    143–45

Alamodome, 18, 26, 49, 180. *See also*
    football dome stadium

  building of, 47–48, 193

    controversies in, 17–18

  first event, 18

  impact, 194

  Krier on, 29

  opening, 18, 193–94

  underground tunnel connecting
    arena and, 28–30

Alarcón, Martín de, 128

Alderete, Eddie, 39, 44

Alemán, Eugenio, 166

Allen, Alma, 79

Amateur Sports Facilities task force,
    218–21, 226–27

Amato, Charlie, 40

Amen, Henry, 120, 121

American Basketball Association
    (ABA), 11, 12

Ancira, Ernesto, 65, 82

Andrade, Hope, 39

Anthony, Pete, 95

Aquifer, Edwards, 52

aquifer recharge protection hearing,
    53

aquifer recharge zone, 50, 52–54, 57,
    59, 62, 205. *See also* Edwards
    Aquifer

arena. *See* AT&T Center

Army Corps of Engineers, 133, 134,
    136, 137, 139, 140, 148–49, 157,
    163, 186

Arneson River Theater, 134

Arts Collaborative, 216–17

AT&T, 160

The mayor of San Antonio from 1991 to 1995, N E L S O N W. W O L F F enacted several major economic developments for the city. He is the author of *Mayor: An Inside View of San Antonio Politics, 1981–1995* and *Baseball for Real Men: Seven Spiritual Laws for Senior Players*. He currently serves as Bexar County judge.

H E N R Y C I S N E R O S is executive chairman of CityView. He has also served as president of Univision Communications and secretary of the U.S. Department of Housing and Urban Development, and he was a four-term mayor of San Antonio.